The Complete Arizona Medicaid and Veterans Pension Benefits Guide

The Who, What, When, Where, and How to Pay for Long-Term Care

Bonus:
"Secrets that Arizona Medicaid and The VA don't want you to know!"

Extended Care, What is it, and How to Pay For It?

Qualify for ALTCS and Protect Your Savings

Bonus: Complete Guide to Veterans Pension with Aid and Attendance Benefits

Extended Care: The What, Who, Why, When, Where and How to Pay For It?

FINDING CARE, VETERANS PENSION, MEDICAID/ALTCS, AND PRIVATE PAY OPTIONS

Then we will discuss how to pay for care, protect your life savings, and avoid disinheriting your family.

Printed in the United States of America

Author Steve Dabbs
7650 S McClintock Rd #103-493
Tempe, Arizona 85283

www.CareFundingSolutions.com

www.VeteransPension.com

www.ALTCS.org

www.ArizonaMedicaid .com

Ordering Information:

Quantity sales. Special discounts are available on quantity purchases by corporations, associations, assisted living communities, and others. For details, contact the "Book Sales Department" at the address above

The Complete Arizona Medicaid and Veterans Pension Benefits Guide / Steve Dabbs —1st ed.

ISBN 979-8-218-07763-1

Dedicated to my wife Cecilia Dabbs, without her support and love, I would have never been able to complete this endeavor.

TABLE OF CONTENTS

"Running away from your problems is a race you'll never win."

Anonymous

PREFACE

Chronic Illness has caused the loss of life savings to millions of seniors, robbing them of the retirement lifestyle they once had.

A needless financial tragedy, one that is avoidable!

Long-Term Care expenses could rob you and your family of your assets, leaving you penniless and your heirs with nothing. The need for long-term care could be responsible for taking your dignity, independence, and pride in your retirement years.

The need for long-term care is a real problem that seniors and Baby Boomers alike face today, and costs are rising as much as twice that of the national inflation rate.

One of the biggest mistakes people make is moving into a community they cannot afford, only to have to move later with fewer resources.

Long-term care planning is essential to avoid making the same mistake that others have.

The information in this book could save you thousands of dollars and hours of undue stress.

Remember, you must act on the information and strategies to benefit.

Without action, there is only *re-action!*

ABOUT THE AUTHOR

STEVE M. DABBS, CMP™, AIF®, CEP®, CLTC®

(Photo of my Basset Hound Charlie and myself. I could hold him in my arms when I started writing this book. Today he weighs 70 lbs.)

Accredited Investment Fiduciary®
Certified Medicaid Planner™
VA Accredited Claims Agent - Accredited by the Department of Veterans Affairs
Financial Planner/ Investment Advisor
Certified Estate Planner™
Certified Long Term Care Specialist™

Steve Dabbs began his working career in the Navy and is a Vietnam veteran. He served on the USS Racine LST-1191.

He entered the financial services industry in 1978. He has been an Investment Advisor Representative since 2011. In 2018 he started "LTC Wealth Management, LLC," a Registered Investment Advisory firm. Dabbs founded the firm with a focus on Long-Term Care Financial Planning.

In 2003, he began helping veterans by educating them on the Veterans Pension with Aid and Attendance benefit program. Then, on June 30, 2011, he became a VA-accredited claims agent, accredited by the Department of Veterans Affairs.

As a VA-accredited claims agent, Dabbs can legally represent a veteran before the Department of Veterans Affairs in preparing, presenting, and prosecuting VA claims.

On August 1, 2012, Dabbs became a Certified for Long-Term Care® - CLTC®

Then, in 2016, he became a Certified Medicaid Planner™, CMP™. To achieve certification, a CMP™ must meet specific education and experience requirements and show proficiency in Medicaid Planning or ALTCS Planning in Arizona.

The fact that Steve Dabbs is accredited by the VA and a CMP™ demonstrates that Dabbs has a solid working knowledge of how the VA Pension program works with Medicaid/ ALTCS and how they conflict with one another.

In 2018, he became an Accredited Investment Fiduciary®, putting Dabbs above the pack. The Accredited Investment Fiduciary® (AIF®) is an ethical certification issued by Fi360.

As a fiduciary, Steve Dabbs is required by law to put a client's best interest first.

Today he is a national mentor, trainer, and consultant on Medicaid/ALTCS planning and Veterans Pension with Aid and Attendance benefits, actively advising financial planners and attorneys throughout the United States.

MY WHY

Steve Dabbs, CMP™, AIF®, VA Accredited Claims Agent

It was a beautiful day in the spring of 2004. I was to speak on a little-known benefit called at the time, "The Veteran's Improved Pension with Aid and Attendance[1]."

In 2004 few were aware of this veterans' benefit.

Once done with the presentation, a lady approached me and inquired, "Can I ask you a question?"

I love to joke with people. I responded, "I'm married if that is your question!" She laughed and said, "No, that's not my question." She continued, explaining, "I recently lost my husband, and we spent all our money caring for him. I now have $25,000 to live on for the rest of my life." She asked, "Is there any way I can go back in time and get these benefits?"

As I looked into her eyes, I saw her sadness and fear. It was the look of fear of running out of money.

I had to say, "No, there isn't, ma'am."

I vowed from that day forward to do everything I could to prevent this from being someone else's story.

INTRODUCTION

Long-Term Care
The What, Who, Why, When, Where, and How to pay for it?
What is Long-Term Care?

Long-term care is helping an individual with their health and personal care.

Long-term care includes both help with Activities of Daily Living; ADLs, and Incidental Activities of Daily Living; IADLS.

Activities of Daily Living or ADLs include eating, bathing, grooming, dressing, transferring, mobility, toileting, and hygiene.

Incidental Activities of Daily Living include shopping, food preparation, housekeeping, laundering, managing finances, medication assistance, using the telephone, and transportation.

Help may be from a friend or family member, a hired caregiver at home, an assisted living group home, or a community.

Who Needs Long-Term Care?

Anybody unable to perform certain everyday functions or activities that a healthy person can do may need long-term care help. There is no specific age range for those who avail of these services, but most of these individuals are over age 65.

Why Consider Long-Term Care?

Aging is the leading cause of the need for long-term care. Over 70% of those over 65 will need long-term care for at least a two-year period.

When Will You Need Long-Term Care?

The need for long-term care can happen at any time to anybody. It can be a gradual progression over time due to aging or happen suddenly due to an accident or stroke.

Where to Seek Long-Term Care?

As the previous paragraphs state, our family members are the first long-term care providers. After they can't provide the level of care needed anymore, who do you talk to, and where to go for care?

What Are the Steps?

First, seek advice. Speak with a Certified Placement and Referral Specialist of CPRS. Secondly, know your needs and accept your need for care.

Then, after you realize it's a necessity, it's time to look for a place. Check the Arizona Department of Health Services website for enforcement actions against them. See azfhs.gov

How to Pay for It?

People usually pay for Long-Term Care from their savings.

Some purchase long-term care insurance to cover a part or all of the expenses. Purchasing insurance can be a heavy financial burden for people who can't afford the premiums.

Many do not have the savings to cover the cost of long-term care over a long period. This is when Medicaid/ALTCS and Veterans Benefits play an important role.

The Perfect Storm.

The cost of long-term care has been dramatically affected by today's out-of-control inflation rate in the United States. The cost increases in the long-term care industry are nearly double that of the inflation rate, with no end in sight. And to make matters even worse, there is also a caregiver shortage as well in the United States.

This makes long-term care planning an essential part of any financial plan.

SECTION I

WHAT IS EXTENDED CARE?

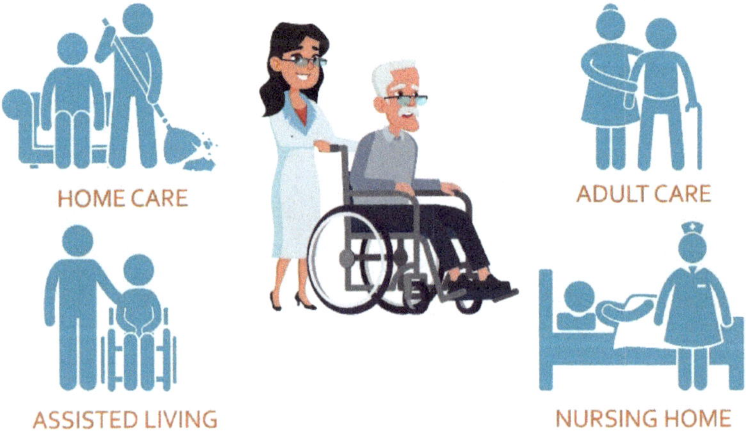

Chapter One

WHAT' S EXTENDED CARE OR LONG-TERM CARE?

Extended Care or Long-Term Care is special assistance with activities of daily living or ADLs.

It is needed because of an illness, injury, disability, or cognitive impairment. Care can be in a nursing home or community, assisted living community, home health care, or community-based care by a family member.

Extended care services range from help with day-to-day activities, such as assistance with:

- Dressing, Toileting - getting up and down and hygiene
- Transferring in and out of bed or chair
- Feeding - cutting up food, Continence care, Bathing
- Cognitive impairment assistance (Alzheimer's or Dementia)
- Mobility, Grooming.

What are the chances this will happen to you?

More than two out of three people in the United States will be caregivers or care receivers!

LET ME REPEAT!

MORE THAN TWO OUT OF THREE PEOPLE IN THE UNITED STATES WILL BE EITHER A CAREGIVER OR A CARE RECEIVER!

Facts and Figures

Alzheimer's Disease Facts and Figures: *Prevalence, Incidence, and Mortality*

As reported by the Alzheimer's Association in 2021

- An estimated 6.2 million Americans age 65 and older will be living with Alzheimer's Dementia in 2021.
- More than 1 in 9 people (11.3%) age 65 and older have Alzheimer's Dementia.
- Two-thirds of Americans over age 65 with Alzheimer's Dementia (3.8 million) are women.
- Deaths due to Alzheimer's between 2000 and 2019 has more than doubled, increasing 145%.
- 1 in 3 seniors die from Alzheimer's or another form of Dementia.

Caregiving

In 2020, more than 11 million caregivers of people with Alzheimer's or other dementias provided an estimated 15.3 billion hours of unpaid care, a contribution to the nation valued at $257 billion.

Nearly half of all caregivers (48%) who provide help to older adults do so for someone with Alzheimer's or another dementia.

Approximately two-thirds of caregivers are women, and one-third of dementia caregivers are daughters.

Forty-one percent of caregivers have a household income of $50,000 or less.

Cost of Care

In 2021, total payments for all individuals with Alzheimer's or other dementias were estimated at $355 billion (not including unpaid caregiving).

Medicare and Medicaid are expected to cover $239 billion or 67% of the total health care and long-term care payments for people with Alzheimer's or other dementias. Out-of-pocket spending is expected to be $76 billion.

Total payments for health care, long-term care, and hospice care for people with Alzheimer's and other dementias are projected to increase to more than $1.1 trillion in 2050.

The total lifetime cost of Care for someone with Dementia is estimated at $373,527.

Ref: Alzheimer's Association see:
https://www.alz.org/news/2021/new-alzheimers-association-report-examines-racial

Long-Term Care is a serious matter.

In fact:

70% of all Americans are expected to need long-term care at some point in their lives. *(National Academy of Elder Law Attorneys)*

For a couple turning 65, there is a 75% chance that one of them will need long-term care. *(The Wall Street Journal)*

Over 70% of people with Alzheimer's live at home and receive 75% of the assistance they need from unpaid caregivers. *(Understanding Alzheimer's, Alzheimer's Association)*

The average annual cost of a private room nursing home in Arizona was $109,026 in 2021 and is expected to jump to over $191,000 by 2040. *(Genworth – Annual Cost survey)*

63% of caregivers use their own retirement and savings funds to pay for care for another person. *(Genworth – Beyond Dollars 2018)*

Conclusion

What are your "denial" and "excuses" for not acting to solve this problem for you and your family?

Do you really want your kids cleaning you and helping you off the toilet? Lifting you out of the bathtub?

Do you want to lose your dignity? Do you want to have the government or nursing home taking your family's inheritance?

I know that this is a little depressing. However, there are solutions to the problem of long-term care.

Please read on. There are answers to the long-term care dilemma.

Chapter Two

WHEN DO YOU KNOW YOU OR A LOVED ONE NEEDS CARE?

What are the signs that you or a loved one may need long-term care?

Deciding to move to an assisted living facility can be difficult.

One of these signs does not necessarily warrant a move, but it may be time to consider a move as they add up.

Moving to an assisted living facility before it becomes mandatory because of a fall or other illness is wiser than dealing with a move because of a health crisis.

Here are 11 signs to watch for in your loved one that indicate the person should no longer live alone.

Yard and House Not Kept Up and Clean

An unclean yard and home might indicate an underlying cognitive issue with our senior parents. For instance, uncleaned spills might signify that our parents have a physical impairment that limits their ability to do simple housecleaning activities.

Additionally, keep an eye out for dust and cobwebs, bathroom mold, moldy refrigerator items, and other house issues. If the home was always clean and kept neat in the past, pay attention to such changes. The inability to tidy up might mean that housekeeping help is needed, or an assisted living facility might be in order.

Depressed and Changes in Mood

Depression and low mood are mental health conditions leading to sorrow and loss of hope. If our loved ones start to have frequent feelings of sadness or emptiness, they lose sleep and pleasure in their everyday activities, and then there is a problem. Depression can affect both mental health as well as physical health.

Hygiene Issues

Poor personal hygiene can be early signs of cognitive issues. Not taking a bath or changing clothes are red flags to look for in your senior loved ones.

Diminishing strength and balance might also lead to poor hygiene in our seniors; this could cause them to fear they may fall while bathing.

These are indicators that it is time for an intervention.

Loss of Mobility

According to the National Institute in Aging, "Older adults who lose their mobility are less likely to remain at home; have higher rates of disease, disability, hospitalization, and death; and have poorer quality of life."

Making sure that your loved one gets adequate exercise, even with a walker or cane, is essential to help keep them healthy and maintain their quality of life. Assisted living helps by offering regular activities and exercise programs.

Memory and Cognitive Decline

Memory loss is not uncommon as we age. It is essential to monitor the progression of cognitive decline and notice signs of memory loss before it advances to diseases like Alzheimer's.

A sign of memory loss is when your loved one experiences confusion about where they are in places they knew in the past or misplaces things and retraces steps to find the lost items.

Your loved one may begin to have poor judgment, be unable to manage a budget, lose track of the date or the season, or have difficulty holding a conversation.

Be sure a properly prepared Power of Attorney is in place long before your loved one becomes incompetent and cannot sign one.

In Constant Pain

Although pain is a common health condition in our seniors, many need maintenance to ease their constant pain.

Care providers in an assisted living facility can monitor pain and manage it, increasing the quality of life for those needing care that is not available in the home.

Driving a Car

It is common today to see seniors driving on the roads. However, there is a point when they start to have problems with mobility, reaction time, and vision. They become a danger to themselves and others.

As our loved ones age, you may need to make some hard decisions and take away their ability to drive. With the help of the state motor vehicle division, you and your doctors may have to make that decision.

Unopened Mail or Mail Left in the Mailbox

Even though the internet has taken on much of the role of the Post Office, letters and other mail are still a basic form of communication and key to daily living.

We all forget to check our mail from time to time, but persistent cases of unopened mail will force you to help sort the correspondence and ensure bills are settled on time.

A Shift in Internet Activities and Habits

Today's technology advancements are wonderful. The internet has put information in our hands that has never been available before.

You should be vigilant to notice changes in internet use and establish solutions for the changes.

Denying or Hiding Problems

Seniors may hide their problems for fear of embarrassment and losing their independence. They start by denying issues and situations that affect them, like falls and physical pain or misuse of pain medication due to potential overdoses.

Multiple Hospitalizations in a Short Period

Multiple hospitalizations, trips to the emergency room, or visits from the local fire department within a short period may signify that your loved one should not be living on their own.

Falls are a common reason for trips to the emergency room for people age 65 and above. Falls are also the number one cause of death for those over age 65.

If your loved one is in this situation, it is time to start a dialog with your them and their doctor. A doctor can help by recommending they not return home from the hospital and must be released to a safe and secure environment.

See website: "Signs it might be Time for Assisted Living"
CarefundingSolutions.com/blog/

Chapter Three

THE PROMISE "I WILL NEVER PUT YOU IN A NURSING HOME!"

A mother of a neighbor had Dementia. I saw them every morning on their front porch, spending time together. They both looked happy.

Then I noticed my neighbor's face was tired and stressed. There were even times I would hear her yelling and angry at her mother. As time passed, she grew more tired because of her mother's worsening condition.

Plus, she was also neglecting both her husband and children.

I once asked her why she kept enduring all the stress. She told me she had promised her father that she would never put his wife, her mother, in an assisted living or nursing home.

We love our senior parents so much, but how can we keep our promise if we cannot keep up with the demands of our day and life's demands?

What comes to your mind as an alternative is hiring an in-home caregiver. There are a lot of home care service providers that you can talk to regarding your parent's condition. You can also hire somebody you know or who is referred by your friends.

However, we can't set aside the fact that our parents' condition can get worse. In this situation, we might need somebody to watch over them twenty-four hours a day, seven days a week, and a home care service is no longer practical. Maybe sending your loved one to an assisted living community or a nursing home would be the best option.

In the end, the promises may need to be broken. Even though you vowed to take care of your elderly loved one, you are living up to your promise by doing what is best for them.

Just because you cannot help them bathe or lift them out of their bed and onto their favorite couch or wheelchair doesn't mean you failed your mother and father.

If helping them to move to an assisted living community or group care home is what is best for them, this will prove that you are keeping your promise to take care of your loved one.

Yes, there are cases of maltreatment and abuse against the elderly in nursing homes. However, the conditions and the services provided in these facilities have already improved over the past few decades, and you should be able to find one that provides the same love and care you are giving your elderly loved one.

To sum it up, it may be ideal for you to take care of your elderly loved ones and keep your promise.

However, if personally taking care of them is impractical and is detrimental to you and your immediate family and loved ones' welfare, it is probably time to break yourself free from your worries and do what is best for them.

Chapter Four

WHAT'S THE RIGHT TYPE OF CARE?

There are four types of care: Home Care, Home Health Care, Assisted Living Community, and Nursing Home Care. How will you know what's best for you?

Home Care

Let's first talk about Home Care. Who should consider this type of care?

Individuals who just need basic care and are not cognitively impaired may stay home and have a caregiver come into their homes. In this scenario, they may seek help from a Home Care service provider which offers non-clinical services ranging from housekeeping to providing companionship and help with Activities of Daily living.

Home Health Care

Another type of care is Home Health Care, or simply Home Health, which provides professional medical services at home to treat illnesses and help recover from a medical condition or injury. Registered health professionals administer it.

This type of care is for individuals with medical conditions or injuries that do not require hospitalization or rehab but still require medical attention and assistance.

Assisted Living Community

At some point, Home Care and Home Health Care may not be viable options due to the higher level of care needed and the cost.

Social interaction is also necessary for a person's well-being.

An Assisted Living Community's big attraction is the social interaction they provide. They have daily planned activities to help their residents stay active and engaged.

Assisted Living Communities give personalized care in a residential setting.

They provide help with both Activities of Daily Living or ADLs and Incidental Activities of Daily Living, which is somewhat similar to what Home Care provides. However, in Assisted Living Communities, medical services are easily accessible whenever needed, and as already mentioned, social interactions through social programs and activities are also encouraged and observed.

This type of care is for people who do not need immediate medical attention but still require monitoring and supervision because of their difficulty or inability to perform their everyday activities.

Nursing Home Care

Unlike Assisted Living Communities, which provide help with everyday activities, Nursing Homes provide skilled/professional medical Care 24/7 by specially trained medical staff. A nursing Home is for individuals who do not need to be in the hospital but cannot be taken care of at home. Nursing Home Care is a much higher care level than an Assisted Living Community.

This may be for short-term rehabilitation or long-term medical care. A Nursing Home is usually for people who cannot take care of themselves independently and require close monitoring and supervision.

Now that we have differentiated these types of care from one another, here are some of the things you may want to consider when you plan to avail of their services and help you choose among them.

The Cost

Hiring a private caregiver to care for things you can't do alone can be expensive.

The average hourly rate of caregivers is $25 (the price varies depending on the place you are in), and they only do the essential home care services such as food preparation, bathing, grooming, running errands, companionship, etc.

Skilled and highly trained home health care professionals that provide non-laboratory medical procedures cost more, ranging from $45 to $85 an hour.

Genworth Financial conducted a survey in 2021 which says the average cost of a semi-private room in a nursing home costs $255 a day.

So, for those who are on a tight budget, it is a cost-prohibited. (See Section IV - Long-Term Care Funding Solutions.)

Chapter Five

HOW TO KEEP A SENIOR LOVED ONE SAFELY IN THEIR HOME

It can be challenging to keep an aging loved one in their home as they get older and start to need more care. You may feel like you're at your wit's end, not knowing how to provide the care your loved one needs while keeping them in their home. Here is a simple guide on how to keep a senior loved one in their home.

Our guide includes tips on finding the proper care, arranging for help, and ensuring your loved one feels comfortable and safe in their home.

Finding the Right Care in the Home

Finding the proper care is essential when caring for a senior loved one. You want to ascertain that your loved ones are getting the care and support they need while also feeling comfortable in their home. There are a few different types of care you can consider:

- **In-Home Care:** In-home Care is a great option for seniors who need a little help with their day-to-day tasks. In-home care providers can help with bathing, dressing, and grooming and can assist with meals, transportation, and medication management.
- **Home Health Aide:** A home health aide is a nurse or a medical assistant who provides care in the home. They can help change bandages, give medication, and check blood pressure.

Making Your Loved One Comfortable and Safe

Once you've found the proper care and arranged for help, you must ensure your loved one is comfortable and safe in their home. Here are a few tips:

- Make sure the home is safe for your loved one. Remove any tripping hazards, install grab bars in the bathroom, and ensure all staircases have handrails.
- Encourage your loved ones to keep a routine, which will help them feel comfortable and safe in their home.
- Create a comfortable space for your loved one. This could be a chair they can relax in, a soft blanket, or pictures of friends and family.
- Make sure your loved one has plenty of social activities. Seniors need stimulation and interaction just as much as anyone else. Suggest joining a club, visiting a library, or visiting a nearby friend.

Take Care of Their Diet

A balanced diet is indispensable to keeping your loved one healthy and strong. Here are a few tips for making sure your loved one is eating well:

- Serve smaller meals more often throughout the day, and this will help them digest food better and avoid feeling tired.
- Make sure the meals are healthy & nutritious. Add plenty of fruits and vegetables, and don't forget whole grains.
- Avoid serving processed foods or sugary drinks.
- Encourage your loved ones to drink plenty of water, which will help them stay hydrated and healthy. This is particularly important in Arizona.

Learn and Practice Mindful Communication

Mindful communication is a form of communication that focuses on being present in the moment and listening attentively to the person you are communicating with one on one. It can be helpful when communicating with a senior loved one, as it can help you better understand their needs and wants. Here are key tips for practicing mindful communication:

- Be patient and take your time. Don't rush the conversation or bombard your loved one with questions. Listen attentively and let them take their time answering.
- Don't assume you know what they're thinking or feeling. Ask questions and genuinely listen to the answers.
- Don't be judgmental. You need to accept your loved ones for who they are and don't criticize their opinions or choices.
- Be supportive. Offer your help and support and be there to listen if your loved one needs to talk.

The Bottom Line

These tips are helpful if you are on the hunt for ways to keep your loved ones at home as they age. Remember that what works for one individual might not work for another, so be sure to tailor the care to fit your senior's individual needs. With some creativity and effort, you can help make your loved one's golden years their best.

SECTION II

HOW – WHAT - WHERE

Chapter Six

TRANSITIONING TO AN ASSISTED LIVING COMMUNITY, WHAT DOES THAT FEEL LIKE?

The Role Reversal Can Be Challenging and Uncomfortable

When your mom or dad is struggling to maintain their independence at home, it is challenging to broach the topic of assisted living.

When we were children, our mom and dad worked hard for our livelihood and wellbeing. While you want to care for them and sacrifice for them in return, you may be overworked, not equipped, or even qualified to care for your aging parent. However, your priority should be keeping your parents or loved ones safe, happy, and protected during their retirement age. This is why it may be time to discuss moving into assisted living.

Are we asking too much of them?

Change is complicated and hard for everybody, and moving to assisted living or long-term senior care is a massive change. Suddenly, you are asking your parents or loved ones to form new acquaintances, navigate unfamiliar schedules, trust professional caregivers, and acclimate to a new environment.

Transition to Assisted Living

The transition from living independently to assisted living can feel daunting, but it doesn't have to be. With your help and a supportive assisted living community, you can make the change smooth with only a few bumps in the road for your loved one.

One of the most significant concerns about transitioning to assisted living is losing independence. However, residents can come and go as they please and make their own decisions at most assisted living communities. They will be able to do the things they love and have plenty of opportunities to socialize with friends and neighbors.

The staff at assisted living communities are there to support your loved one, and they will work with you and your loved one to create a care plan that meets their personal needs. The staff helps residents with many day-to-day needs, from managing medication to getting dressed in the morning. And you will have peace of mind knowing that someone is always there to help your loved one if needed.

The First Step

If considering transitioning a loved one to assisted living, take a tour of your local communities and see what they offer. You will be able to meet the staff and residents and feel what life your loved one would be like in the assisted living community or group home.

Once you find a couple of places you think your loved one would like, make arrangements to have your loved ones go with you to tour the community.

How to Deal with Problems in Assisted Living. Making the Emotional Transition to Assisted Living.

When deciding to move into an assisted living community, it's important to remember that there will be an emotional transition period. This is a time when your loved one may feel a range of emotions, including sadness, loneliness, confusion, and even anger. It's important to allow them time to grieve the loss of some of their independence and the life they knew.

It's also important to remember that assisted living is not a nursing home, and they will still have many of the same freedoms and independence they enjoyed before moving.

Assisted living communities help your loved one maintain as much independence as possible. There will be staff on hand to help your loved one with tasks such as bathing, dressing, and grooming, but you will still be able to come and go as you please.

The staff at assisted living communities understand that making the transition can be difficult, and they will do everything they can to help make the process as smooth as possible. They may provide support groups or counseling services to help you adjust to your new life. Remember, you are not alone in this process, and many people have gone through the same thing and can offer advice and support.

Many have welcoming communities made of volunteers from the community to help make the transition a positive experience.

Tips to Make the Transition to Assisted Living Easier

Making the transition to assisted living doesn't have to be complicated. Here are a dozen tips to help make the process smoother:

1. Don't Wait Until the Last Minute

   The earlier you start planning for assisted living, the easier the transition will be.

2. Do Your Research

   Many different assisted living options are available, so take the time to find one that's right for you.

3. Talk to Your Family and Friends

   They may have personal experience with assisted living and can offer valuable advice.

4. Consider Your Budget

   Assisted living can be expensive, so ensure you have a realistic idea of what you can afford.

   I see this all too often when I get a call and the family member starts with "Mom and Dad are about to run out of money." This can be avoided with proper planning and being realistic about the actual cost of an assisted living community or group home.

   As you know, one of my passions is acting as a financial planner and am a Certified Medicaid Planner. I can help to develop a Long-Term Care Financial Roadmap™.

   The Long-Term Care Financial Roadmap™ looks at all the stress points of your financial situation and will help to ensure that the community you decide to move into is also one you can afford.

5. Ask Questions

   The more you know about a particular community, the better informed your decision.

6. Consider Your Loved One's Needs

   Assisted living may be the best option for them if they're struggling with daily activities.

7. Weigh the Pros and Cons

   Assisted living isn't suitable for everyone, so consider all the pros and cons before deciding.

8. Talk to the Staff

   They can answer any questions and provide more information about the community or group home.

9. Ask for References

   Talk to other residents and their families to get an idea of life at the community or group home.

10. Make the Transition Gradual

    If possible, move to assisted living gradually rather than all at once. Many communities and group homes have respite programs that allow you to have a short-term stay in the community. This will help make the transition smoother for everyone involved.

Conclusion

If you or a loved one is nearing the age where assisted living might be necessary, starting planning and researching what that will look like is essential. The process can seem daunting, but it doesn't have to be with the help of the right resources. We hope this blog post has helped give you an idea of what to expect and some tips for finding the perfect community for your needs.

Chapter Seven

HOW TO FIND THE RIGHT ASSISTED LIVING COMMUNITY?

WHAT IS A CERTIFIED PLACEMENT AND REFERRAL SPECIALIST?

How do we find the right assisted living community for our loved ones?

Here are some things you should do and the factors you want to consider when choosing the right Assisted Living Community.

1. Check the Background of the community through the Arizona Department of Health and Human Services. This can be done on their website at AZDHS.gov.
2. Read online reviews of the community. Do this before you flop down a non-refundable deposit!
3. Learn what services and amenities are offered by the community.
4. Get an answer: Can the community meet your loved one's needs and care requirements, not just now but as their health changes in the future too?
5. What is the proximity of the community to you? Location may not seem like a big deal, but the closer your loved ones are to you, the more frequently you'll visit them.
6. Is the cost of the community affordable? Not just now but as the cost of care and rates increase in the future.

7. Assisted living inflation rates are as much as double the Consumer Price Index rate. This is because food and energy costs are not used in the CPI calculation.

Finding the information and answers to these questions can be a hassle, especially for people considering an assisted living community due to the lack of time to care for their loved ones properly.

Once you find a community that seems to meet the needs of your loved one, you may not be able to know for sure if the community is the right place until your loved ones move into the assisted living community. But by then, it is too late. Moving again is disturbing and stressful for your loved ones and you.

Should You Seek Professional Help with These Questions?

Some organizations have this information and answers to all these questions. And they can help you to choose the place that will suit your loved one's condition and preference. But this can take a lot of time and may be difficult to discern. This is why many turn to certified professionals like Certified Placement and Referral Specialists and Certified Medicaid Planners™

What is a Certified Placement and Referral Specialist, and how can they help you answer your many questions? A Senior Placement Agent provides placement services for people seeking an assisted living community for themselves or a loved one.

A competent senior placement agent will talk to the person needing care and their family and ask for their living preferences, medical needs, location, and budget. With this information, they can recommend what type of assisted living condition fits best.

Problems with Senior Placement Agents

A senior placement agent plays an important role in the assisted living industry. But unlike other professionals that have governmental oversight like the insurance industry, securities industry, medicine, and the legal profession, placement agents are not regulated by any governmental agency.

This lack of oversight has led some to make unsuitable and inappropriate recommendations regarding senior placement. In some severe cases downright dishonest!

Industry leaders created PASRS or the Professional Association of Senior Referral Specialists to address these issues and self-regulate placement agents. Today they are called the National Placement & Referral Alliance.

The NPRA developed the "Certified Placement and Referral Specialist designation or CPRS."

Since senior placement agents are unregulated, it is hard to say how many people are out whizbanging around in Arizona doing placements.

The most common infraction is churning. In the securities and insurance industry, churning is where the agent frequently buys and sells stocks or replaces insurance products just to make another commission on the transaction. **The unscrupulous placement agent also churns.**

This practice of churning has given the senior placement agent a bad reputation. Causing some assisted living communities and group homes to not pay for placement.

The Certified Placement and Referral Specialist has agreed to meet a higher standard and "Best Practices."

Chapter Eight

HOW DO YOU KNOW A LOVED ONE IS RECEIVING THE BEST CARE?

Worried About the Care Your Loved One Is Receiving?

You're not alone. Millions of families are in the same boat, trying to make sure their loved ones are being cared for properly. It's hard to know what's going on when you're not there. That's why we've put together this list of signs that will help you know if a loved one is getting the best possible care.

1. The Care Community Is Clean and Well-Maintained

A dirty, cluttered, or poorly maintained care community signifies that your loved one may not be getting the best care. The staff at a suitable care community will take pride in their work and keep the environment clean and organized.

2. The Staff Is Friendly and Knowledgeable

The staff at a care community should be friendly and welcoming to both you and your loved one, and they should also be knowledgeable about caring for elderly or disabled people. If the staff is rude, unhelpful, or uneducated, it may signify that the care community is not a good fit for your loved one.

3. The Staff is Attentive and Responsive

Good care facilities have staff who are attentive and responsive to the needs of their patients. If the staff is slow to respond to your loved one's needs or seems apathetic, it may tell you that the care community is not meeting their needs.

4. The Care Community Has a Good Reputation

One of the best ways to determine whether or not a care community is good is to look into its reputation. Ask your friends and family, do some online research, or call the community directly to ask about their services. If the care community has a good reputation, they are likely providing good care to their patients.

5. The Care Community Offers a Variety of Services

An excellent care community will offer a variety of services to meet the needs of its patients. These services may include nursing care, physical therapy, occupational therapy, speech therapy, social activities, and more. If the care community you are considering does not offer all of the services your loved one needs, it may not be the best fit.

6. The Staff-to-Patient Ratio

The staff-to-patient ratio is an important consideration when choosing a care community. A trustworthy care community will have a staff that is adequately staffed to meet the needs of their patients. If the care community you consider has a high staff-to-patient ratio, it may be a sign that your loved one is not getting the individualized care they need.

7. The Care Community Has Good Customer Reviews

Another good indicator of a care community's quality is its customer reviews. Good care facilities will have positive reviews from past and current patients.

8. The Care Community Has a Good Safety Record

A reliable care community will have a good safety record. This means that the staff is adequately trained to handle emergencies and that the community is safe for patients. If the care community you are considering has a history of safety violations, it may be a sign that your loved one is at risk.

9. The Care Community Has Good Financial Stability

The care community you choose should be financially stable. This means that they have the resources to meet the needs of their patients now and in the future. If the care community you are considering is having financial difficulties, it may be a sign that they will not be able to meet the needs of your loved one.

Choosing a care community for a loved one can be a daunting task. By looking for the ten signs of a good care community, you can ensure that your loved one is getting the best possible care.

Final Thoughts

It can be challenging to know when our loved ones need help, especially if they live far away. But there are some key signs you can look for to make sure they're getting the best possible care. By being aware of these signals, you can put your mind at ease and feel confident that your loved one is in good hands.

SECTION III

VITAL INFORMATION YOU SHOULD HAVE

Chapter Nine

CARING FOR THE FAMILY CAREGIVER

What Is a Caregiver?

According to Merriam-Webster, a caregiver is a person who provides direct care (as for children, elderly people, or the chronically ill).

Challenges of Being a Caregiver to a Parent

Being a family caregiver is challenging and is certainly no walk in the park. This is especially true if you have other things to do, like a job or go to school.

Sometimes, it is so overwhelming that you don't know how to manage your time to perform all the things you need to do. You have to allot time, sometimes it requires extra, to provide care for a loved one. It exhausts your strength and patience at times, especially when the person you are taking care has a hard time taking instructions. You repeat instructions over and over, and most of the time you end up doing it for them.

Caregiving is not only about providing assistance with grocery shopping, running errands, housekeeping, and preparing food. A caregiver's tasks sometimes include transfers from bed to a chair, bathing, toileting, making appointments with the doctor, and administering medicine. All the demands of being a family caregiver cause both stress and guilt.

What Is Caregiver Stress?

Caregiving not only exhausts your physical strength but is also draining emotionally. A lot of caregivers tend to be more irritable due to emotional exhaustion.

What Are the Signs of Caregiver Stress?

Caregiver Stress is a serious problem among caregivers and those they are taking care of. It not only affects the person themselves, but it also affects the person they are in charge of.

If the caregiver is having problems, they will not be in good shape to tend to all the needs of the person who needs their care. They tend to be tardy or absent at times, act slower or feel lazy because they don't feel well, get angry easily because they are emotionally exhausted, and so many other things can go wrong if a caregiver is stressed. These are some signs that a caregiver is stressed:

Caregivers who are stressed may sleep too much to cope with the physical exhaustion they experience every day. If you are going to take a look at it, it really is the normal reaction of the body to recover from a hard day's work. But if it's becoming more frequent, then it's not normal.

Gains or losses of weight easily can be a sign your body is overtaxed. If you have swings in weight or a sharp weight gain or loss, this could be a sign you need to focus on your own health.

Alcohol or drug abuse. Sometimes, when you are living a stressful life, you want to escape to a state where you are worry-free and without a care in the world. Many people, even caregivers, seek this through alcohol and a few from drugs. They usually get irritated easily, and there are some episodes of mood swings, and this is due to the emotional stress they get without something to let it out.

Caregivers who are stressed are often unhealthy due to the neglect of their own health.

Chapter Ten

HOME CARE VS HOME HEALTH CARE

"Home Care" and "Home Health Care" seemed so similar, but they are two different types of services.

To further understand Home Care and Home Health Care, these are the key differences:

Home Care

- Provides "non-clinical" or "non-skilled" care by professional caregivers.
- Helps with everyday tasks like bathing, dressing, grooming, cooking, cleaning, and transportation. It does not include medical care like nursing or therapy.
- Continues as long as you want, based on your budget and needs.
- Typically paid directly by the patient or long-term care insurance. Medicaid may also cover home care.
- Family members and professional caregivers provide home care services.
- Helps patients 24/7, depending on the patient's budget and needs.
- Home care is typically provided at home.

Home Health Care

- Licensed nurses and therapists provide "clinical" or "skilled" care.
- Services are more medical. Home health aides can help with things like bathing, grooming, and dressing until you can safely do them again or have a caregiver who can safely assist you. But the focus of care is skilled nursing and therapy.
- It continues as long as your doctor certifies the need.
- Medicare, Medicaid, and most private insurance plans for eligible patients are covered.
- The home health team is made up of skilled professionals such as nurses and therapists.
- Visits are typically a few hours per week, depending on the patient's needs and doctor's orders.
- Patients can receive home health care in their place of residence, including assisted living facilities and group homes.

What is the Difference in Cost?

According to a survey conducted by Genworth Financial, the average cost of in-home care in the US is $4,481 a month based on 44 hours a week of care, while for Home Health Care, the cost is higher at an average of $5,148 a month.

However, since Home Health Care can include nursing services, it is more economical than skilled nursing care, which averages over $9000 monthly for a shared room and $9,034 for a private room.

To sum this up. Home Care assists an individual's everyday activities when they can no longer perform them. On the other hand, Home Health Care is more focused on assistance with medical needs. These are two different types of care, and your needs will determine which one you should receive.

Chapter Eleven

HOSPICE AND PALLIATIVE CARE

What Is Hospice Care?

Hospice Care focuses on the comfort and quality of life of a person with a terminal illness, attending to their emotional and spiritual needs.

To receive Hospice Care, a patient must decide to stop life-prolonging medical treatments. They do so because the side effects outweigh the benefits. Hospice Care prioritizes comfort and quality of life by reducing pain and suffering.

Who Qualifies for Hospice Care?

Doctors usually order Hospice Care when care goals shift away from aggressive treatment of a specific disease or illness to relieving symptoms such as pain, shortness of breath, anxiety, restlessness, nausea, and vomiting. Anyone with a terminal diagnosis who doctors feel has a life expectancy of six months or less.

There are Four Levels of Hospice Care, These Are:

- Routine Hospice Care - the most common and frequently used level of Hospice Care. In Routine Hospice Care, the patient receives care at their place of residence, which can be in an assisted living community, a nursing community, or their private home.
- Continuous Hospice Care - the care provided by the hospice team for between 8 and 24 hours a day to alleviate pain and address acute medical symptoms. The services must be

focused on nursing care in conjunction with hospice aid services which are provided to enable the terminally ill patient to remain at home during a symptom crisis.

- Inpatient Hospice Care - This level of care controls the pain or other acute symptom management provided in a nursing home or other designated inpatient setting. General Inpatient Care is provided to patients who have symptoms or pain that cannot be managed in an outpatient setting. General Inpatient Care requires a registered nurse available 24 hours a day to tend to the patient's needs.
- Respite Care - this is available to temporarily lessen a patient's primary caregiver of some of their daily responsibilities. Respite care is often provided in a hospital, hospice inpatient community, or a long-term care community that has sufficient 24-hour nursing staff present.

Hospice Care can be provided anywhere the patient considers home. It can be in the comfort of their own homes or in nursing facilities.

What Does It Mean When You Are in Hospice Care?

Hospice Care is for people who are nearing the end of their lives, some also call it "End-of-Life" Care. But this doesn't always mean death and loss of hope. It's just that the doctor has set the expectation of life. Many people still live much longer than six months. Some even live for years after their diagnosis. You can also stop and restart Hospice Care anytime.

You might be thinking that Hospice Care means that your doctor stopped the medical care you need and has given up on you. Which is not the case. The service simply focuses on the quality of your life instead of trying to cure your medical condition.

What Is Palliative Care?

On the other hand, Palliative Care helps people with serious illnesses to feel better by preventing or treating their symptoms and side effects. Palliative Care aims to help people alleviate their condition and feel better.

Palliative Care also treats emotional, social, practical, and spiritual problems that illnesses might bring up. Once they feel better in these aspects, it is observable that their health condition gets better as well.

Who Qualifies for Palliative Care?

Palliative Care is for people of any age and at any stage in an illness, whether that illness is curable, chronic, or terminal. If you or a loved one are suffering from a medical condition that might need Palliative Care, be sure to consult your doctor and ask for a referral for a consultation for this type of care. It may be offered to people with illnesses such as cancer, heart or lung disease, kidney failure, Dementia, HIV/AIDS, ALS (amyotrophic lateral sclerosis), etc.

Both Palliative Care and Hospice Care provide comfort. But Palliative Care can begin with diagnosis and treatment of the medical condition. Hospice Care begins after treatment is stopped and when it is clear that the person will not survive the present medical condition.

SECTION IV

WAYS TO PAY FOR EXTENDED CARE

Ways to Pay For Extended Care:

- You pay with your current income and life savings, and other assets.
- You ask a family member or friend to pay for care.
- Funds from a reverse mortgage
- Long-Term Care Insurance
- Use your life insurance - Life Settlements
- ALTCS - Medicaid Long-Term Care Benefits
- Veterans Pension Benefits

Let's take each one and discuss the various options.

Chapter Twelve

PRIVATE PAYING FOR CARE, PAY WITH YOUR INCOME AND PERSONAL FUNDS

Fourteen percent of those in the United States use their current income to pay for long-term care, including life savings, home sale proceeds, and other assets. Some turn to family and friends to help pay for care.

It is noteworthy that less than 5% of the US population over 65 has a net worth of $1 Million. Source: US Census Bureau, Survey of Income and Program.

Consider this:

- By 2029, 54% of seniors in the middle-class will not have the means to pay privately for needed care.*
- If married, paying for long-term care could leave their spouse without sufficient funds to live on the rest of their lives.
- If single and private paying for care, you could make the assisted living community or the nursing home community your heir.

Think about this question; Do you want to rely on family and friends to help pay for care?

**2019 study by Caroline F. Pearson, Charlene C. Quinn, Sai Loganathan, A. Rupa Datta, Beth Burnham Mace, and David C. Grabowskian, aging researchers at NORC, a nonpartisan research organization based at the University of Chicago.

Chapter Thirteen

MEDICARE INSURANCE COVERS EXTENDED CARE – RIGHT?

Medicare and Medicaid - although similar sounding, are very different in what they cover and how to qualify for them.

As a Certified Medicaid Planner, I often cringe when I hear Medicare pays for long-term care. It does not!

Though both healthcare programs are government-sponsored, we hear people use these two names interchangeably or take one for the other.

Each program is governed by its own set of rules and regulations. In addition, they cater to the needs of the person and are designed to benefit different groups.

It sometimes happens that some people may fulfill the eligibility criteria of both Medicare and Medicaid. In that case, these individuals are dually eligible for both programs.

To make the right choice and to navigate through the complex maze of rules and regulations of both programs, you need to understand both Medicare and Medicaid. Let's get started.

What Is the Difference Between Medicare and Medicaid?

Medicare and Medicaid differ from each other in more points than one, though both programs were created in 1965 and they are both funded by taxpayer money.

Medicare is based on age, and the program is managed by the federal government. On the other hand, Medicaid is both federally and state-funded but is governed by the individual states and considers the income of the applicant to assess eligibility. Of course, there are a few more differences, and some exceptions too.

What Is Medicare?

Medicare is a federal program that provides medical coverage to two groups of American citizens. So, who is eligible for Medicare?

- Individuals aged 65 and older
- People with certain disabilities

Medicare is a primary medical coverage insurance program that helps millions meet certain healthcare costs. The program has four parts, covering different medical services such as doctor visits, hospitalization, rehabilitation after a three-day stay in the hospital, and prescription drugs.

What Is Medicaid?

Managed at the state level but is a joint federal and state program. Medicaid is designed to cover long-term care and certain healthcare services for Americans in the low-income group.

The eligibility, services, and regulations differ slightly from state to state. Hence, the program might be managed under different names in different states.

Beneficiaries of Medicaid receive healthcare services at no cost at all or a lower cost under certain circumstances. Beneficiaries must recertify each year to remain eligible to receive Medicaid benefits.

Who Is Eligible for Medicaid?

- People 65 and older with income within limits
- People with disabilities, including blindness
- Pregnant women

- Children (aged 19 or less) with disabilities
- Individuals who meet income and assets eligibility criteria

What Does Medicare Cover?

Medicare coverage is divided into four parts. The following is a brief overview of the four plans.

Part A: Hospital Insurance

This part of the Medicare program pays for hospital stays and inpatient care. Regardless of the income, this plan covers everyone aged 65 or over.

To qualify, either the spouse or beneficiary must have paid the Medicare taxes for 10 years, at the least.

In the case of Part A coverage, although coinsurance and deductibles apply, most beneficiaries are not obligated to pay a premium for these services.

Part B: Medical Insurance

Part A - the hospitalization coverage - is just a small part of Medicare. Part B covers other essential services related to healthcare.

Medicare Part B pays for doctor visits, outpatient surgeries and care, disease screening services, flu shots, medical tests, including x-rays, accessories such as walkers and wheelchairs, etc.

The beneficiaries pay a premium for Medicare Part B services. The premiums are taken from the individual's Social Security payments or similar programs.

For individuals earning up to $91,000 annually, the premium is around $170.10. Individuals who earn more have to pay a higher premium for Part B coverage.

In addition, like in Part A, coinsurance and deductibles apply here as well.

Monthly Premium: $170.10

Part C: Medicare Advantage Plan

Part A and B are part of the original Medicare plan. The other two parts - Part C and D - are offered by private insurance companies approved by Medicare.

Part C or the Medicare Advantage Plan covers both hospitalize-tion (of Part A) and medical services (of Part B). In addition, this plan also pays for dental treatment, hearing and vision care treatments, and prescription drugs.

One of the main advantages of this plan is that the beneficiary can save costs on medical services purchased privately.

Premium: Changes with plan

Part D: Prescription Drug Coverage

Individuals can consider joining Part D if their Part C plan doesn't cover prescription drugs.

The beneficiaries of Plan D are required to pay monthly premiums. In addition, an annual deductible and copayments for certain prescription drugs also apply.

Premium: Changes with plan

Because Medicare does not pay 100% of your medical bills, choosing the right Medicare supplement or Medicare Advantage plan is extremely important.

Be careful before you drop your traditional Medicare supplement plan to move to a Medicare Advantage plan that looks inviting.

Medicare Advantage plans for some can make sense, but for others they are a financial mistake.

It would be best to speak to a qualified Medicare advisor, not a Medicare supplement or advantage salesperson only interested in a commission.

What is that old saying? "Buyer beware!"

How Much Will Medicare Pay for Long-Term Care?

Some wrongly believe that Medicare also covers long-term care after hospitalization or otherwise. They are wrong. Medicare's long-term care coverage is minimal and only for a short period of time.

Medicare doesn't pay for long-term care!

Long-term care includes services that fulfill personal care needs. Long-term care is not always medical-related. It also includes bathing, dressing, feeding, taking care of the beneficiary's hygiene, and helping with a person's daily living activities.

Again, Medicare doesn't cover custodial care (long-term care). Instead, the program provides limited skilled nursing care.

Skilled Nursing Care: Medicare will only pay for the costs of skilled nursing care for the first 20 days, after a minimum of a 3-day hospital stay. After the initial period, the individual has to contribute around $185 per day (2021) toward coinsurance. Medicare will cease to pay for skilled nursing care after 100 days.

Home Health Care: Medicare pays for certain skilled care services to individuals who are homebound due to injury or illness. The doctor treating the individual must agree that skilled care (therapy, nurses, etc.) is required. Here too, the contribution of Medicare is limited. The program will pay for only 28 hours of skilled care per week.

Hospice: The program pays for hospice care for terminally ill patients. For Medicare to cover hospice services, the doctor must provide a certificate that the individual might not live longer than six months. To extend the coverage after six months, the doctor must certify the patient is still terminally ill.

What Does Medicaid Cover?

As Medicaid is state-managed, the benefits, as well as the program name, vary by state. Nevertheless, the states are obligated by the federal government to include certain compulsory services.

Medicaid benefits are grouped under two categories: Mandatory and Optional. Let's check some of the benefits under each category.

Mandatory Benefits

- Home care services
- Family planning services
- Midwife services
- Nursing facility services
- Outpatient hospital services
- Disease screening services like x-ray, scans, etc.
- Laboratory services
- Counseling services to quit tobacco for pregnant women
- Transportation (related to the hospital, doctor visits, etc.)

Optional Benefits

- Therapy services for language, hearing, and speech disorders
- Dental services
- Case management
- Home maintenance services
- Recreation services
- Travel and transportation services (not related to medical care)
- Personal assistance
- Hospice services
- Personal care
- Physiotherapy and chiropractic services
- Respiratory care services
- Prescription drugs
- Eyeglasses

The Medicaid program funds certain much-needed essential services omitted from Medicare. The program covers the costs of nursing care or other related care services for people who have no means to pay for them.

How to Qualify for Medicaid

Medicaid is the largest source of healthcare coverage in the U.S. The program covers more than 70 million Americans.

The beneficiaries pay almost nothing for government assistance. In rare instances, some individuals will have to make copayments for some of the benefits. Since Medicaid costs almost nothing, there are strict eligibility requirements that may vary by state.

The Affordable Care Act that was introduced to expand the coverage of Medicaid so that more adults could gain eligibility uses the Modified Adjusted Gross Income (MAGI) methodology to assess financial eligibility.

That said, the older method of using income methodology adopted by SSI administrators still applies to people who are 65 or older, disabled, or blind.

Medical Qualification

Individuals who require assistance to fulfill some or all of their daily needs will qualify for Medicaid.

In addition, the program will also cover people suffering from dementia disorders such as Alzheimer's or who require constant skilled nursing care.

Generally, the assessor would determine medical eligibility by checking the number of ADLs (activities of daily living) the applicant needs assistance with. Applicants who require nursing home level care will qualify for Medicaid.

Financial Qualification

The administrators will look at the income and assets to determine the eligibility of the applicant.

Individuals applying for Medicaid assistance must have a monthly income not exceeding $2,523 (for 2022). The income of the healthy spouse of the married applicant is not considered to check eligibility.

Medicaid also reviews the assets (or resources) to determine eligibility. To qualify, the applicant must have countable assets of value less than $2,000.

Non-countable assets such as residence (one home), vehicle, irrevocable funeral plans, and burial plots are excluded from scrutiny.

Non-Financial Qualification

To receive Medicaid benefits the individual must be a resident of the state or plan to stay in the state for a considerable period. American citizens and certain qualified non-citizens are eligible to apply for Medicaid.

What Does It Mean to Be Qualified for Both Medicaid and Medicare?

If an individual is over 65, he/she may qualify for both Medicaid and Medicare. People who qualify for both programs are known as duals or dual-eligible beneficiaries.

They are members of Medicaid (with full benefits) and Medicare Part A and/or Part B. They may also qualify to receive Medicare Advantage Plan (Part C). The dual-eligible people are divided into two groups: Full Duals and Partial Duals.

In the case of full duals, the Medicaid program covers all long-term health care services that are not provided by Medicare.

Individuals with low income and asset levels (below the eligibility limit) become fully dual-eligible. They receive all Medicaid benefits offered by their state.

For beneficiaries in the partial duals group, Medicaid covers certain expenses incurred under Medicare. Medicaid will pay for Part B (of Medicare) premiums.

If applicable, Medicaid will also cover premiums for Part A of Medicare. In certain scenarios, the state-managed Medicaid program will also pay for copayments, coinsurance, and deductibles.

The partial duals group comprises people who receive income and possess assets higher than what's prescribed by Medicaid but less than 125% of the Federal Poverty Level (FPL).

How Are Medicaid and Medicare Funded?

Medicare and the means-tested Medicaid form the largest social healthcare program in the world.

They serve millions of people in the United States. These programs make health care services affordable to millions of people, especially the elderly, disabled, and those in the low-income groups.

Medicare is a federal program and Medicaid is a joint federal-state program managed by the state. Since they are government-sponsored, both Medicare and Medicaid are indirectly funded by the people - the taxpayers. The Medicaid program is financed by the federal and state governments.

The U.S. Treasury has instituted two trusts to fund Medicare. These are the Hospital Insurance Trust Fund and Supplementary Medical Insurance Trust Fund.

These trusts are funded using money received as payroll taxes from the self-employed, employers, and employees. Other sources that fund these trusts include premiums, taxes from social security benefits, and interest earned on trust investment. Periodically, Medicare and Medicaid receive additional funding from the federal government.

Final Thoughts: How Do the Two Programs Differ?

To put it in a nutshell, Medicaid is a social welfare program, whereas Medicare is an insurance program.

Hence, to receive Medicare, the beneficiary must pay a monthly premium directly or through payroll taxes when employed.

In contrast, Medicaid beneficiaries need not pay premiums for the benefits.

Like other social welfare programs, Medicaid is funded by federal and state governments using taxpayer money.

If you are under age 70 and concerned about how you will pay for long-term care, you might want to look into long-term care insurance while you can still afford it.

Chapter Fourteen

LONG-TERM CARE INSURANCE – WHAT'S NEW?

Long-Term Care Insurance: The Why, Who, What, When, and Where

Long-Term Care Insurance is not a new insurance product; it was first offered in the early 1980s and has evolved over time, recently gaining popularity. This is due in part to product advancements, pricing stability, and the fact that the life expectancy of people in the United States has increased considerably.

The average life expectancy was around 65 just half a century ago; today, a considerable percentage of the population is expected to live up to 85 or longer. (ref. 2019 Social Security Actuarial Life Table)

A growing number of people, especially the baby-boomer generation, are approaching the stage of life when they might need long-term care.

By 2030, all baby boomers will be 65 or older; this tsunami of people turning 65 puts a strain on government long-term care programs like Medicaid – ALTCS and Veterans Pension benefits programs, making long-term care insurance even more expensive and more important to have in place.

Long-term care isn't a topic that aging parents or their children like discussing. No individual wants to lose independence and rely on children, relatives, and friends for daily activities, such as bathing and dressing.

The fact that you are on the CareFundingSolutions.com site indicates that long-term care insurance is on your mind. **This may**

be because a loved one or friend has required long-term care, and you are more aware of the need for long-term care insurance.

Source: www.CareFundingSolutions.com

Long-Term Care Insurance is not like other insurance policies; deciding to purchase long-term care insurance is both emotional and financial.

Here you can learn solid facts about Long-Term Care Insurance - benefits, drawbacks, costs, services, and more - before deciding whether to purchase long-term care insurance.

The What, Why, Who, When, and Where of Long-Term Care Insurance

What is Long-Term Care Insurance?

As you age, general weakness and health problems become common. You might require help performing day-to-day activities that you now take for granted.

Long-term care insurance helps pay for the services associated with personal and custodial care. These care services assist elderly and disabled people with the activities of daily living (ADLs).

Long-term care insurance covers care services in various settings, including nursing homes, assisted living facilities, community living centers, and in-home care services.

Long-term care insurance also covers care coordination, cooking, bathing, dressing, feeding, and medication management.

Long-term care insurance policies reimburse for a wide range of services. Many long-term care insurance companies allow you to pick and choose policies that offer the benefits specific to your needs.

Many people in their 70s and primarily 80s need long-term care.

However, regardless of age, medical conditions such as a stroke, heart attack, or early onset of cognitive disorders such as Alzheimer's and Parkinson's will precipitate the need for assistance with activities of daily living.

Disability due to accidents might also necessitate services covered by long-term care insurance.

Why Should You Consider Long-Term Care Insurance?

It would be wise to consider long-term care insurance because the latest statistics on this subject say so. And the numbers don't lie.

According to the latest report by The Administration for Community Living, approximately 70% of people who live past 65 will need long-term care.

On average, men will need long-term care support for 2.2 years, whereas women will require such services for 3.7 years. As much as 20% of the 65+ population will need long-term care for more than five years.

More than anything, owning a long-term care policy offers peace of mind.

Long-term care insurance is a lot like having fire insurance. You don't want or expect a fire incident to burn down your home, but having home insurance that covers fire damage will put you at ease and give you the confidence to meet the expenses if such events happen.

Comparing the Risk:

- **Life insurance:** 100% of us will die at some point, so the need for life insurance is self-evident. It is not a matter of if you need life insurance, it is how much life insurance do you need.
- **Health insurance:** Unless you are incredibly unusual or extremely wealthy, you will have a need for health insurance coverage throughout your life.

- **Automobile Accident insurance**: one out of every 240 people will have an auto accident and need car insurance.
- **House fire insurance**: one in every 1,200 homes will experience a fire.
- **Long-term care insurance: one out of two people will need long-term care.**

One in 1200 homes experience a fire, yet one out of two people will need long-term care insurance.

100% of people that own a home have fire insurance and would never consider not having coverage, yet only 22% of individuals own long-term care insurance.

To the question of how confident those are who own long-term care insurance about paying for long-term care if the need for such care arises, nearly 92% of people who had long-term care insurance answered they were totally confident or somewhat confident in their purchase.

Who Should Consider Long-Term Care Insurance and Who Should Not?

Long-term care insurance is for everyone except those with high fixed incomes.

If you are sandwiched between the extremely rich and extremely poor, then long-term care insurance is the best, and in most cases the only, option for paying for long-term care.

Who Needs Long-Term Care Insurance?

1. People who have an Average to Above Average Net Worth

Most people prefer not to depend on their children and family for physical help as they get too frail to perform certain activities of daily living.

Paying for care out-of-pocket is out of the question unless you are a multimillionaire. Expenses for long-term care services can quickly wipe out your family's savings in no time.

The average cost of some long-term care services in the United States as of 2020 is as follows:

- The annual cost of a private room in a nursing home is $105,850 and in Arizona is $96,353 per year, per ALTCS Arizona Medicaid.
- Homemaker services and health aides charge around $150 per day or $35 per hour in Arizona.

Several factors influence the cost of long-term care services. How much you'll end up paying will depend on the type of care, the duration, and where you live.

You need to have a considerably large nest egg to pay out-of-pocket for your long-term care needs.

2. People Who Don't Qualify for Medicaid

Medicaid dominates any discussion on long-term care, as it currently pays for 42% of long-term care costs in the US. However, many do not know that a large chunk of the population in the United States won't qualify for the government-sponsored long-term care program without advanced Medicaid Planning.

The state-managed Medicaid program provides personal and custodial care for people in the low-income group.

To qualify for Medicaid, you need to prove you receive an income less than the limit prescribed by the state government and that your countable assets have a value less than what's mandated by Medicaid.

Compared to Medicaid, long-term care insurance is more flexible. Plus, long-term care insurance is more liberal in covering in-home care services. Best of all, you can choose where you want to receive care.

This is the most significant negative with ALTCS or Medicaid. Not every care facility accepts ALTCS at the same time, and all

communities, nursing homes, group care homes, and home care agencies take private funds to pay for care.

People with long-term care insurance can also benefit from the Medicaid program. With the state "Long Term Care Partnership Program," an applicant can preserve assets and still qualify for ALTCS or Medicaid long-term care benefits.

3. People Who Already Have Regular Health Insurance

Long-term care insurance and regular insurance are like chalk and cheese. Most services paid for by long-term care insurance are not medical in nature.

Most LTC policies are comprehensive. They cover personal care such as bathing, dressing and feeding, therapy, including physical, speech and rehabilitation, and skilled nursing care.

Some LTC policies also cover homemaker services along with personal care services.

Health Insurance Does Not Pay for Long-Term Care

Health Insurance

Some people believe a regular insurance policy would cover long-term care costs. Health insurance coverage for long-term care is limited, if at all. In most cases, health insurance like Medicare and commercial or private health insurance policies pay only for skilled care for a short period of time.

- Regular insurance covers skilled care only if the requirement for such care follows recent hospitalization.
- Health insurance will pay only if the requirement is for skilled medical care. In the case of long-term care insurance, the services are not always medical in nature.
- Most health insurance policies do not reimburse for personal or custodial care.

Medigap, Medicare Supplements, and Medicare Advantage Plans ("Supplements")

Supplement plans were introduced to make up for some of the shortcomings of Medicare. These programs pay for certain services not covered by Medicare. Supplements help individuals:

- Pay for deductibles and copayments
- Pay for short-term nursing home stays when the hospitalization is covered by Medicare
- Extend your doctor and hospital coverage

Like Medicare, supplement plans do not pay for long-term care services.

Disability Insurance

Your disability insurance won't pay for long-term care either. Moreover, most of these policies won't provide any benefits after age 65.

Disability insurance supplements income to make up for the loss of pay due to any disability.

As you can see, regular insurance is no substitute for long-term care insurance.

How Much Does Long-Term Care Insurance Cost?

The cost of the policy varies from one insurance provider to another. How much you'll pay also depends on factors such as:

- Your age at the time of purchasing the long-term care insurance policy.
- The coverage and the benefits you need.
- The type of long-term care policy you choose.

The insurance company may hike your policy's premiums in the future, where you have no option but to pay the increased premium.

That said, once the coverage begins, you are not required to pay premiums for the duration of the LTC.

Keep in mind, you can write a little check to an insurance company now or write a big check to an assisted living community later!

When Does Long-Term Care Coverage Begin?

Policyholders need to satisfy two essential criteria to receive benefits.

The Benefit Trigger

Insurance companies use the 'benefit trigger' to determine whether you qualify for assistance. The process involves filing an assessment form by a social worker or nurse.

The insurance carrier appoints the assessment worker who would determine your eligibility based on the severity of cognitive impairment or your ability to perform Activities of Daily Living (ADLs).

In most cases, the company will decide to pay if you need help performing two or more ADLs.

The Elimination Period

Long-term care insurance beneficiaries will not receive assistance as soon as the benefit trigger occurs. The beneficiary has to wait for a short duration - called the elimination period - before receiving payment for LTC services.

It's up to the beneficiary to decide the elimination period when choosing the policy. The elimination period could be anywhere between 0 to 365 days.

You - the beneficiary - will have to pay out-of-pocket for personal and custodial care services during the elimination period.

When Should You Buy Long-Term Care Insurance?

There are still many who think of long-term care insurance only after the need arises. Timing is crucial in long-term care insurance.

Those who wait too long to purchase a long-term care insurance policy will face high premiums. **Some become ineligible due to a pre-existing medical condition, so don't wait until it is too late.**

The other extreme of buying too early has some drawbacks. When purchasing too early, the policyholder has to pay premiums for a long time before becoming eligible to receive benefits.

Is there a best age to buy long-term care insurance? According to The American Association for Long-Term Care Insurance, the sweet spot - the ideal time to buy long-term care insurance - is in a person's mid-50s to early 60s.

Many experts second this recommendation even though most claims occur when the policyholders are in their 70s, 80s, or even 90s.

The following two points will convince you to abide by the organization's recommendation.

- Roughly 23% of all applications of people in their 60s are denied by insurance companies. This is nearly double the policy applications denied to people in their 50s.
- Although the Affordable Care Act prevents insurance companies from excluding applicants with pre-existing health problems, the rule doesn't extend to long-term care policies.

If you are over 65, a <u>Short-Term Care</u> program may be a smart alternative to long-term care insurance.

What Are the Different Types of Long-Term Care Insurance?

People looking for long-term care insurance now have more choices than ever. That said, long-term care insurance can be broadly classified into two main types.

1. Traditional Long-Term Care Insurance

The traditional or stand-alone policy offers the most coverage for your dollar.

The policy gives you greater control over your future. At the same time, it protects your family and friends from the impact of your long-term care needs. Traditional Long-Term Care Insurance has been available for decades and has the following components:

- To purchase a policy from an insurance company, you need to be in reasonably good health.
- You have to pay a premium from the time you purchase the policy. The premiums can be paid monthly, quarterly, semi-annually, or annually, depending on the insurance company.
- When you file a claim, you have to prove you are cognitively impaired (suffering from Parkinson's or Alzheimer's) or require assistance with at least two ADLs.
- If you never require or claim benefits, neither you nor your heirs can collect any payment from the insurance company.
- The insurance company can increase premiums in the future. Some insurance companies may give you the option to pay the increased premium or retain the same premium but with reduced coverage (fewer benefits) under the same policy.
- The elimination period can range from 0 to 365 days.
- The benefits period generally ranges from two to six years depending on the insurance carrier.
- Nowadays, most policies under this category cover nursing home and in-home care services.
- Some policies allow you to include additional benefits such as coverage for home modification, allowing a family member to provide in-home care, or hiring a care manager.

The policy you purchase will specify how the insurance company will pay.

Cash Benefits Policy: The Company will pay the full daily benefits, and you need not show proof of care services received.

Indemnity Policy: The Company will pay the daily benefit upon proof that at least one care service was received per day.

Reimbursement Policy: You submit receipts or other documents proving you paid for care services out-of-pocket, and the company will reimburse you up to the maximum daily benefit limit.

2. Modern Asset-Based Long-Term Care Insurance

Asset-based long-term care insurance is fast gaining popularity because of the flexibility it offers. Some also refer to it as a hybrid long-term care plan.

As the name suggests, this type of policy generally combines two types of coverage under one plan.

For example, companies can offer a hybrid policy that covers both life insurance and long-term care. Alternatively, the policy could be a combination of an annuity and long-term care plan.

Such policies are called asset-based because they are funded with your savings, home equity, retirement account, or a wide variety of different assets.

How Does Life Insurance-Based Long-Term Care Work?

In a life insurance policy, after death, the company pays the death benefit to your heirs or anyone nominated as the beneficiary.

The beneficiaries can use the death benefit to pay for funeral expenses, clear debts, or fulfill any financial needs.

If you have the hybrid plan, you could, when the need arises, use the death benefit money to pay for your long-term care.

If you never claim the long-term care benefits, the money will be paid to the nominee after your death.

How Does an Annuity-Based Long-Term Care Work?

An annuity is also an insurance contract. In an annuity contract, you either pay a lump sum amount (once) or make periodic payments (monthly or annually, depending on the insurer).

The beneficiary can choose a policy that starts making payments immediately. In contrast, as in long-term care insurance, the beneficiary can fix the benefit payment to start at a later date.

Depending on the policy, the payment will be made for a fixed period or until the beneficiary's death.

In annuity-based long-term care, at the time of the beneficiary's death, any money remaining under the policy will be passed to the heirs.

Where and From Whom Should You Buy Long-Term Care?

It should be clear by now that long-term care insurance is quite different from other forms of insurance. It's as important as health insurance, but a lot more complex.

Hence, once you make up your mind to buy long-term care insurance, the next logical step is to decide where and from whom to buy it.

The biggest mistake that most people make is to approach a non-certified insurance agent or broker.

Sadly, most of them do not possess the necessary qualifications. They are not trained to handle the complexities of such policies or advise about long-term care insurance products impartially.

If you are making a long-term care plan for yourself or a loved one, the first and most important step is to engage a specialized advisor.

One way to ensure you get the best and unbiased advice on the subject is to approach an agent with a CLTC designation.

A professional with a CLTC designation will help you understand and plan long-term care as well as advise on the best long-term care insurance policy that would suit your needs and the best insurance carrier who offers the policy.

Certified in Long-Term Care (CLTC) is the long-term care insurance industry's first professional designation. The certification program was launched in 1999 by The Corporation of Long-Term Care Certification. The program remains the only third-party-issued LTC certification.

Here are six more reasons to engage a long-term care insurance advisor with a CLTC designation:

(a) Long-term care insurance professionals with a CLTC designation do not focus on selling a product. Rather, they help create a comprehensive plan for your long-term care to protect your physical, financial, and emotional well-being.

(b) An insurance professional with a CLTC designation is well-versed in the technical aspects of long-term care and a variety of other programs such as Medicaid and Medicare.

(c) Professionals with a CLTC designation are also trained in interpersonal skills. Since long-term care in most cases is a family affair, a matter of trust, and a subject filled with emotions, the advisor must be competent to carry out difficult conversations with clients.

(d) CLTC is one of the most popular certification programs recognized by most insurance carriers. The CLTC designation is acknowledged by several online financial portals and major national publications.

(e) CLTC is an independent, third-party designation not affiliated with any insurance company. In addition, insurance professionals with a CLTC designation are expected to adhere to a strict code of conduct that would boost trust and credibility.

(f) CLTC-designated professionals are expected to stay abreast of the latest changes and developments in the field of long-term care insurance. The professionals are required to renew their designation by taking a CLTC renewal course every two years.

Conclusion

The fear of losing control over life and depending on others to fulfill basic daily needs can shatter the peace of mind of any person. Everyone needs a plan to meet the challenges of old age.

Although there are many options, such as Medicaid, long-term care insurance is by far the best option for affording quality long-term care.

Long-term care insurance ensures your independence and protects you and your loved ones from the financial, physical, and psychological challenges that might arise in the future.

Even though you think you'll never need long-term care, it's best to be prepared.

Chapter Fifteen

VETERANS BENEFITS

The Veterans Administration provided approximately $ 5.1 billion in 2021 to eligible veterans for long-term care-related care and services.

Source: VA.gov

Compared to the overall spending for long-term care, this is only 1.2% of the total spent on long-term care nationwide.

This low percentage provided by the VA may be due to veterans' and surviving spouses' overall low utilization rate. Much of the low utilization rate is due to a lack of awareness by potential beneficiaries.

The program is far from new; the US Congress passed it into law in 1789 to help disabled veterans and their dependents who fought in the Revolutionary War.

Then, on August 29, 1959, the Veterans' Pension Act Of 1959 was signed into law by President Dwight D. Eisenhower. The legislation revises the non-service-connected pension programs for veterans of World War I, World War II, the Korean conflict, and their widows and children.

Program awareness has increased over the past 20 years, mainly because of a joint effort by insurance professionals, financial planners, and the assisted living industry helping to spread the word.

The Veteran Pension was previously called the Veterans Improved Pension with Aid and Attendance; in 2018, the Veterans Administration formally changed the name to Veterans Pension.

The program's name may be part of the reason for the lack of awareness, the name of the program has the word "Pension" in it. This often confuses veterans. Most associate the word pension with retirement income received from previous employment.

As is with the military, someone must serve 20 years to receive a full pension for their service.

So, I often will hear, "I was only in for four years, not twenty. I don't qualify for a pension."

A better name would be "The Veterans Long-Term Care Program" or "Vets LTC Benefits."

Then, to add to this issue of qualified veterans and their surviving spouses not applying for benefits, many are told they do not qualify when indeed, they do.

I still remember when I was just getting started helping veterans with the "Veterans Improved Pension" program. I went down to the VA Regional in downtown Phoenix to ask them some questions on some cases I was involved with at the time.

I had 5 or 6 files with me and had different questions for each. For the last one, I started my question with, "I have a surviving spouse of a veteran." Before I could ask my question, he says, "*If she makes more than $1,100 per month, she does not qualify!*"

I remember when this happened, I just dropped my head, counted to 10, and then said, "That is not my question."

Understand that his statement was **100% incorrect** because he failed to ask for her unreimbursed medical expenses. This includes any home care and assisted living expenses.

Unreimbursed medical expenses are used to offset income. So, in this case, she was spending $4,200 per month on care, giving her a negative $3,100 net income. So, income is not a bar from getting Veterans Pension benefits.

I left that day baffled why the VA would have someone with his perceived authority and knowledge answering questions for the general public.

I wondered how many people have gone down to the VA Regional Office to learn if they qualify for benefits and met with him and got misinformation. Then walked away thinking they didn't qualify, yet they did. Sad, very sad indeed, but it happens all the time.

Here is another excellent example of some who are poorly trained and are putting out misinformation at the VA.

I was asked to speak to an assisted living homeowners association on another occasion. I was one of four speakers, and one of the other four was someone from the same VA, Phoenix. I accepted on one condition—that I would go first because I had to leave for another engagement.

I went to the meeting location early to set up and place my brochures on all the chairs.

A lady walked over to one of the chairs and picked up one of my brochures to read.

Suddenly she states in an angry tone, "I'm with the VA. Her demeanor was curt, and she came across as ready for a confrontation. I was still going from chair to chair, placing my brochures, so I was leaning over the chair. I looked over my glasses and just said hi, not showing much care who she was.

She said, "Your brochure says that you're a VA Accredited Claims Agent. What's that?" I didn't appreciate her negative tone, so I tilted my head a little, sneered with my eyes, still bent over, so looking over the rim of my glasses, I responded, "You don't know?" *Meaning you don't know what an accredited claims agent is, and you are with the VA? Really?* I thought.

That silenced her for a moment. She continued to review my brochure, then a few minutes later, she blurted out, "There aren't pension benefits for a living spouse!" Again, I didn't like this woman's negativity, so I responded, "Yes, there is." I suppose she was correct because it technically falls under the Veterans Low Income Pension Benefit.

But it is also technically a benefit for a living spouse who needs care, and the cost of her care reduces the household income below the income limit. This is a lot of jargon to say "benefits for a living spouse."

She called me, to her credit, followed the call up with an email the next day, and apologized for challenging me. She said I was right, that there is a benefit for living spouses that need care, and being a VA claims agent is a big deal, she acknowledged.

I have multiple stories like this; much of the misinformation surrounding the Veteran Pension program comes directly from inside the VA.

If this may have happened to you, and you don't even know it. You may be eligible for benefits to help pay for needed extended care if you meet all three "Ms" of "The 3 Ms to Veterans Pension Qualification."

VETERAN PENSION SECRET # 1

You can qualify for both compensation and veteran pension benefits.

Suppose you have a 100% rating and need another individual's assistance and qualify for the Aid and Attendance portion of the benefit. In that case, you can be eligible for additional money to help pay for your care. If you have less than a 100% rating, you get the higher compensation or pension amount or higher of the two.

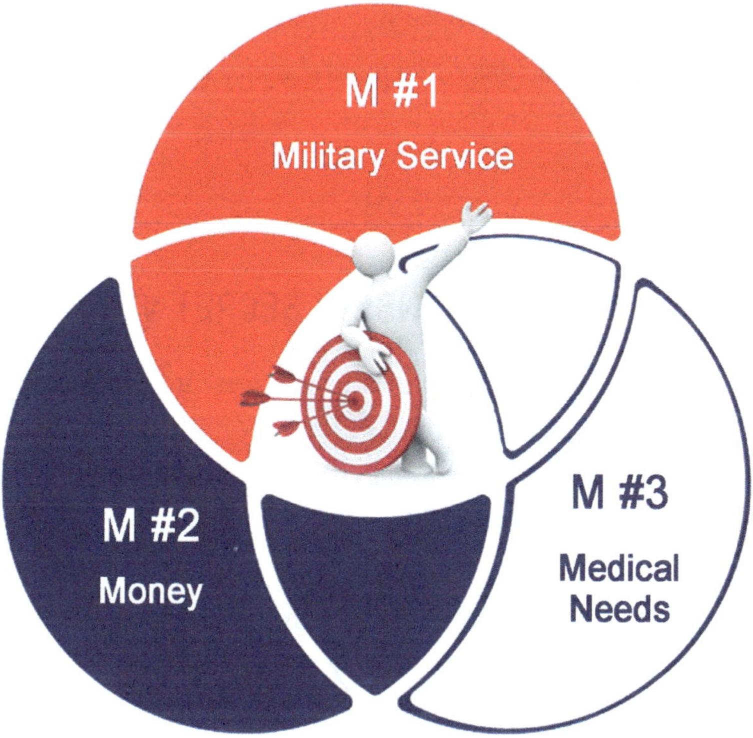

The First M is Military Service:

A veteran must have served at least 90 days of active duty, with one day during a war period, and have an honorable discharge to be eligible for benefits.

The periods of war include:

World War II: 12/07/1941 to 12/31/1946
Korean War: 06/27/1950 to 01/31/1955
Vietnam War: 08/05/1964 to 05/07/1975*

**For veterans who actually served in the war zone, called "boots on the ground" their start date is 02/28/1961*

Gulf War: 08/02/1990 to present

Gulf War veterans must have two years of active duty to qualify; the two years are accumulative.

VETERAN PENSION SECRET # 2

You don't have to have been in the war zone to qualify. You only need to have been in the military during the war period.

For instance, someone serving in the United States or Germany during the Vietnam war would qualify.

The Second M is Medical Need:

A claimant must need assistance from another individual with at least two activities of daily living or ADLs: bathing, dressing, ambulating, toileting, transferring, and eating.

The VA considers medication management as an activity of daily living or ADL for someone with cognitive impairment.

Let's break down these ADLs and how the VA looks at them for qualification purposes.

Bathing: Unlike Medicaid/ALTCS with the Veterans Pension, assistance with bathing doesn't have to be someone physically hands-on bathing you. It can be stand-by assistance because you're a fall risk or need reminders to take a bath because you have Dementia.

Grooming: is also helpful for claims approval if noted by the Doctor completing the evaluation, VA form 21-2680.

Dressing: Like bathing, for dressing to qualify as an ADL, you don't have to have someone putting on and taking off your clothes. Someone with Dementia may need reminders to change their clothing, which will qualify as an ADL for the benefit.

Someone with arthritis may need help butting a button or tying a pair of shoes. All of these will qualify dressing as an ADL.

Ambulating or walking: Walking as an ADL has been on and off for Veterans Penson as a qualifier. I have had claims both approved and denied, with ambulating as one of the two ADL's. When someone at the VA denied one of my claims with just bathing (stand-by assistance only) and ambulating as the ADLs. This came as a complete surprise to me because not a week later, I had a claim approved that was just like the one that was denied.

I called the VA to find out the problem with the claim. The VSR (Veteran Service Representative) said it has always been that way. Ambulation is not an ADL, he told me.

So, check with your claims agent at the time you are filing a claim to know if ambulating will qualify as an ADL.

Currently, it is - see our website carefundingsolutions.com for an updated status on ADLs

Toileting: Toileting includes help getting down and up from the toilet. It's also help with personal hygiene, cleaning oneself, and incontinence care.

Transferring: Transferring is needing help getting up from a bed or chair to a wheelchair or help to a walker.

Eating: Eating can also be the need to be reminded to eat for someone with Dementia. They can be a choking risk and need their food cut up for them. **Cooking is not an ADL**.

Your Doctor's Role

The VA relies solely on what your doctor states on the VA form 21-2680.

If your doctor says you are a fall risk, you are a fall risk. If they say you have early onset of Dementia and you need medication management, then you need medication management, period.

The VA will not question your doctor's authority.

It is always best to have the doctor report reviewed by an Accredited Claims Agent before it is sent in to ensure it is completed properly before the VA receives it.

VETERAN PENSION SECRET # 3

Complete the doctor's report and ask the doctor to sign it. If they object, then give them a blank one and ask them to complete it.

They will take one look at the blank one and sign the other one.

The Third M is Money:

What are the income and asset limits?

The VA calls this limit the "Bright-line limit." For 2022 the bright-line limit is $138,489. It is a combination of all household income and assets.

As mentioned, income is offset by unreimbursed medical expenses.

The limit changes on December 1 of each year. See our website for the current "Bright-Limit."
CareFundingSolutions.com/veterans/

Let's first define countable and non-countable income and assets.

Important to note the VA counts all marital household income and assets as jointly owned.

Income

Countable income includes: Social Security Income(s), all pension income, earned income from employment, **interest income**, RMD's from retirement accounts, short and long-term capital gains, and even **gifts to you from your children to help pay for care is considered income.** Payments from any source unless specifically excluded. The following sources of income are counted for the purposes of completing the financial assessment.

VETERAN PENSION SECRET # 4

There is not a set income limit per se, this is because income is offset by unreimbursed medical expenses.

<u>Deductible Medical Expenses:</u> Unreimbursed medical expenses reduce countable income for purposes of increasing pension benefits. In order to be deducted from income, out-of-pocket non-reimbursed medical expenses must exceed 5% of the VA Maximum Annual Pension Rate for the previous year.

Income Limits: In order to qualify for the full pension benefit, your income must be less than your out-go for unreimbursed medical expenses and cost of care.

Example 1: If you are a married or single veteran with a household income of $4,000 per month, and your cost of care in an assisted living community is $4,500 per month, you would have a monthly shortfall of $500. Therefore, you would qualify for the full monthly benefit.

Example 2: If your income is $4,500 per month, but your cost of care in an assisted living community is only $3,500 per month, you would have a $1,000 positive income.

Now, even though you have a $1,000 positive income, you would still qualify, but only for a partial benefit. The benefit amount paid is determined by subtracting the $1000 from the maximum benefit to get the partial benefit amount. I have purposely simplified and left out parts of the income and out-go. The VA uses a more detailed MAPR equation than intended for this book.

Just understand there is not a set income limit per se. You need to spend your income on care in order to qualify for benefits.

See Maximum Annual Pension Rate or MAPR if you want a more detailed explanation. This can be found on our website.

THE CATCH 22

How do you pay for care to qualify for Veterans Pension if you don't have the Veterans Pension benefits to pay for care?

Classic Catch 22! For some, this presents a real dilemma. How can they use all of their income to pay for care? They have food bills, housing, and utility bills to pay.

If they have savings, they can use the savings until the VA benefits are approved. Since it is a retroactive benefit paid back to the first of the month following the month the claim was submitted. If you submit a claim on January 20, the benefits will accrue from February 1. So, once the lump sum benefits are paid, you can put it back in your savings.

But what if you have no savings? How do you pay for needed care if you don't have the money from the VA to pay for care?

This is less of a problem if you are in an assisted living home or community. The cost of assisted living is considered a medical expense. So you could consider moving from your home. Since an assisted living cost is all-inclusive, it includes room and board, utilities, food, and in some cases, cable.

So now you get the care and reduce your income with other expenses not otherwise included.

Another solution is to apply and get approved for a partial benefit, then once approved, dollar for dollar up to the maximum benefit that you spend on care will be paid and reimbursed by the VA.

Here is what I mean, I once got a claim approved for $1.39! Woo-hoo! I know what am I bragging about, a $1.39 benefit award? Why? Here's why the veteran was approved. Now they can get more home care and increase the care hours over time to maximum benefit.

VETERAN PENSION SECRET # 5

The cost of an assisted living community and a group home is offset by income.

So, if your income is too high to qualify, move to a lovely room with a better view or move to a nicer community.

HOW MUCH MONEY DOES THE VA PROVIDE?

The Total 2022 Veterans Pension with Aid and Attendance Benefits.

The benefit is TAX-FREE and doesn't affect your Social Security benefits or taxes.

Single Veteran.................................... $2,051
Married Veteran................................ $2,431
Surviving Spouse.............................. $1,318
Married Couple Both are Veteran........... $3,253

Housebound Benefit with one dependent: Living Spouse who needs care but the veteran cannot provide the required care...$1,610

See our website for current rates
CareFundingSolutions.com or VeteransPension.com

VETERAN PENSION SECRET # 6

Finance the cost of care till your benefits come in, then use the back money or accrued benefits to pay off the loan. Some companies specialize in this type of financing; see our website for details.

VETERAN PENSION SECRET # 7

The VA allows a family member other than a spouse to be paid to provide care. I have often used a family member as a paid caregiver to reduce the income so the claimant will qualify for a full benefit. But why not the spouse?

I have often said this, "*You married him, now you got to take care of him!*" when asked this question in a seminar by a spouse in attendance, "Can I be the paid caregiver."

The VA assumes you will provide care to the veteran at no charge since you are married. Again, on the other hand, a daughter or other family member or friend can be a paid caregiver. Income must be reported to the IRS. (Talk to a CPA or tax specialist.) Rates should not exceed the going rate in your area for care.

Surviving Spouse Qualification Requirements

First and foremost, understand this is a veteran's benefit, and to be eligible as a surviving spouse, you must have been married to the veteran at the time of their death and not remarried.

The "**D**" in Divorce = **Denied**. If you divorced the veteran, you are not eligible.

Marriage under VA rules: Must be married for at least one year prior to death.

The VA does allow for common-law marriages if the veteran lived in states that recognized common-law marriages. These are Colorado, Iowa, Kansas, Montana, New Hampshire, Oklahoma, Rhode Island, South Carolina, Texas, and Utah. Also, the District of Columbia.

As mentioned, the surviving spouse cannot have remarried after the veteran's death unless the following marriage (last marriage) is with a qualified veteran.

An exception to this rule. If the surviving spouse remarried after the veteran's death and was subsequently terminated either through death or divorce before November 1 of 1990, and the surviving spouse does not remarry, then the surviving spouse would be eligible for benefits. See 38 CFR § 3.55

VETERAN PENSION SECRET # 8

The surviving spouse can continue to pursue a claim for her deceased husband and receive the accrued benefits postmortem. Also, if they need extended care, the date of claim is the veteran's date of death for the surviving spouse. This date is held for up to one year from the date of death.

Can I qualify in the home using a home care agency?

Yes, of course. Just keep the income out-go ratio in mind to determine how many hours of care you will need to reduce your income to qualify for the full benefit.

VETERAN PENSION SECRET # 9

Someone on hospice can get their claim expedited. Send proof to the pension center along with your claim or update your claim and the VA is required to expedite the process.

HOW TO FILE A VETERANS PENSION CLAIM

I will never forget this; I was at the VA Regional Office on Central Avenue. I would often go there at the end of each month to get my veterans "Intent to File a Claim" form 21-0966 officially date stamped.

A young woman came to the counter while waiting for the person to help me. She said, "I'm the daughter of a Vietnam Veteran and have been elected by my siblings to help get my father's Veteran's Pension claim filed; I have no idea what forms are needed or what to."

The VA employee turned and walked to the forms cabinet and said; As she reached for the form, *"I think you will need this one. And I think you will need this one, and I think you will need this one."*

I knew the lady assisting her by her first name and often enjoyed seeing her. She was so friendly and genuine, and she would even give me a friendly hug when I got there. It was all I could do to keep my mouth shut.

I did not want to embarrass her or make any comments. But in my mind thought, "YOU THINK? What do you mean YOU THINK you need this one!"

By the way, this is the same place the Air Force Sergeant was that I mentioned at the beginning of this section.

So, here are the forms I *KNOW* you will need to file a claim:

Veteran's Claim:

___ 1. VBA 21P-527EZ
___ 2. A copy of the marriage certificate.
___ 3. Complete marital history for both veteran and spouse.

Surviving spouse of a veteran claims:

____ 1. VBA 21P-534EZ
___ 2. A copy of the marriage certificate.
___ 3. Complete marital history for both veteran and spouse.

Minimum needed with main claim forms for both veteran and surviving spouse.

___ Certified Copy of the Discharge Papers
___ Copy of most recent bill from care community, group home, or care provider.
___ Physician Evaluation. VBA-21-2680
___ VA Form 21-0969

Additional evidence needed for a surviving spouse of a veteran.

___ Copy of veteran's Death Certificate
___ Marriage Certificate & Complete Marital History
___ Voided Check

Claim forms can be mailed to:
Department of Veterans Affairs844-51
Evidence Intake Center
PO Box 4444
Janesville, WI 53547-4444
Or Faxed 844-531-7818

VETERAN PENSION SECRET # 10

The VA Loses Claims!

I know, unbelievable, but it's true. I remember once I sent in four claims together in the same express mail envelope. Three got put in the system and the fourth was lost.

You will get a letter from the VA in about two weeks notifying you that the VA has received your claim.

So be sure to check on the claim. After a couple of weeks, you can call 877-294-6380 or 800-827-1000

Getting Help Filling Out a Veterans Pension Claim - The Law!

What the LAW States!

Appropriately done, a claim can be approved in three to four months for a veteran and five to six months for a surviving spouse. I have had claims approved in under five days. *(Don't count on that.)*

Done wrong; it can take a year or longer or even be denied.

Let me just say this I THINK, you should consider seeking the help of an Accredited Claims Agent.

They will help and do not charge to Prepare, Present or Prosecute the claim.

They are allowed to charge for these areas: Extended Care financial planning and estate planning if qualified, crisis and non-crises planning, and long-term care financial planning if they are licensed financial planners.

Note that not all accredited claims agents have the knowledge and expertise in other areas.

Steve Dabbs is a Certified Medicaid Planner™ - CMP™, A Certified Estate Planner - CEP®, hold a Certified in Long-Term Care® - LTCi® designation and an Investment Advisor Representative, and lastly, an Accredited Investment Fiduciary®, AIF®.

Cecilia Dabbs is also a Certified Medicaid Planner™ - CMP™, and A Certified Legal Document Preparer.

She is the owner of Legal Document Solutions, LLC and is legally able to prepare Estate, Medicaid and VA planning documents for this process.

They are also allowed to charge a disinterested third party to file a claim. This would be someone other than an immediate family member.

VETERAN PENSION SECRET # 11

Who Can Legally Prepare, Present and Prosecute a Claim for a Veteran or Surviving Spouse?

Myth: A common myth about VA Pension Benefits is that anyone can help a veteran with a claim.

I often learn about unauthorized people who make unsuitable recommendations while helping veterans with the claims process. These individuals are constantly breaking the law.

Fact: The law says that anyone can help a veteran with one claim. Helping someone "one time" can be misunderstood.

Title 38 CFR § 14.630 (a) states that any person may be authorized to prepare, present, and prosecute one claim. This allows a family member or friend to help a veteran with a lawsuit.

This is clarified under Title 38 USC § 5901:

"Except as provided by section 500 of title 5, no individual may act as an agent or attorney in the preparation, presentation, or prosecution of any claim under laws administered by the Secretary unless such individual has been recognized for such purposes by the Secretary." These are the people recognized by the Secretary.

VA Accredited Attorneys, VA Accredited Claims Agents**, Veteran Service Officers

The VA added to the explanation in their Fast Letter 06-26: "Representation before VA consists of actions associated with the preparation, presentation, or prosecution of claim for a VA claimant ... Among other things, representation includes counseling on veterans benefits, gathering information necessary to file a claim for benefits, preparing claim forms ..."

This is violated by many well-meaning advisors, particularly those who are counseling on VA benefits and gathering information. Advisors cross the line as soon as they go from providing general education on VA benefits to answering specific questions.

Questions include whether a veteran will qualify based on their current medical needs, wartime military service, or if they have too many assets. This is a direct violation of the intent and spirit of the law.

I call these individuals that are knowingly violating the law VA Pirates. Beware of these individuals; **If someone is willing to openly break the law with this matter, what else are they willing to do?**

If you are a health care professional, home health provider, assisted living community or group homeowner or director, or senior placement agent. Be sure that the VA recognizes the person you are referring to is an Accredited Claims Agent, Veteran Service Officer, or VA Accredited Attorney.

If you want to see if the Secretary of Veterans Affairs authorizes the person you are working with to help veterans, see:
https://www.va.gov/ogc/apps/accreditation/

VETERAN PENSION SECRET # 12

Contact your Congressional Representative

Your claim can get hung up for several reasons. All US Congress Representatives have a Veteran Liaison in their local and DC offices. They can help to get the claim pushed forward.

VETERAN PENSION SECRET # 14

The Intent to File a Claim

You can lock in the date of a claim with the "intent to file a claim" form 21-0966.

If the VA gets the 21-0966 on or before the last day of the month, the following first of the month will be the date of claim.

So, for example, if the VA receives the from on January 30, then February 1 will be the date of claim. Once approved, the benefits will be retroactive back to February 1. And you have up to one year to send in a formal claim.

So, be sure to do that as soon as you can.

But be careful that the assets are not above the Bright-line limit when you send in the Intent to File. If you are unsure, you should discuss this with your VA claims agent before sending it to the VA.

INDEPENDENT LIVING AS AN UNREIMBURSED MEDICAL EXPENSE

VETERAN PENSION SECRET # 15

Many believe this is not true. But I will let you know that it is not only true, but I have prepared hundreds of claims for veterans living in independent communities.

The main key here is you have to have the need for the assistance of another individual with at least two activities of daily living and be paying for needed care, which is the same that is required for an Assisted Living Community.

Lastly, the Independent Community must provide 24/7 staffing and be considered a safe and secure environment.

It sounds simple enough, but these claims can be more challenging to approve. So, working with a Claims agent that understands this type of claim makes a lot of sense.

VIETNAM VETERANS

Approximately 2.7 million men and women served in Vietnam. Most successfully readjusted to postwar life. Others continue to suffer from a wide range of life-adjustment problems, like PTSD.

During the Vietnam War, the United States used over 19 million gallons of herbicides and crop destruction chemicals, Agent Orange. Anyone who physically served in Vietnam from January 9, 1962, to May 7, 1975, is presumed to have been exposed to Agent Orange.

Those included are also: (Source VA.gov)

"Blue Water Navy" Veterans. These are Navy veterans that served within 12 nautical miles of Vietnam.

"Brown Water Veterans" are veterans who served aboard smaller river patrol and swift boats that operated on the inland waterways of Vietnam

Korea

Veterans who served in a unit in or near the Korean Demilitarized Zone (DMZ) anytime between September 1, 1967 and August 31, 1971.

Thailand

U.S. Air Force veterans who served on Royal Thai Air Force (RTAF) bases near U-Tapao, Ubon, Nakhon Phanom, Udorn, Takhli, Korat, and Don Muang, near the air base perimeter anytime between February 28, 1961 and May 7, 1975.

U.S. Army veterans who provided perimeter security on RTAF bases in Thailand anytime between February 28, 1961 and May 7, 1975.

U.S. Army veterans who were stationed on some small Army installations in Thailand anytime between February 28, 1961 and May 7, 1975. However, the Army veteran must have been a member of a military police (MP) unit or was assigned a military occupational specialty whose duty placed him or her at or near the base perimeter.

C-123 Airplanes

Veterans (including some Reservists) who state that they flew on or worked on a C-123 aircraft between 1969 and 1986.

Other Potential Agent Orange Exposures

Veterans who may have been exposed to herbicides during a military operation or as a result of testing, transporting, or spraying herbicides for military purposes.

Learn about herbicide tests and storage outside Vietnam. https://www.publichealth.va.gov/exposures/agentorange/locations/tests-storage/index.asp

Presumptive Diseases Associated to Agent Orange

AL Amyloidosis
A rare disease caused when an abnormal protein, amyloid, enters tissues or organs

Bladder Cancer
A type of cancer that affects the bladder where urine is stored before it leaves the body

Chronic B-cell Leukemias
A type of cancer that affects white blood cells

Chloracne (or similar acneform disease)
A skin condition that occurs soon after exposure to chemicals and looks like common forms of acne seen in teenagers. Under VA's rating regulations, it must be at least 10 percent disabling within one year of exposure to herbicides.

Diabetes Mellitus Type 2
A disease characterized by high blood sugar levels resulting from the body's inability to respond appropriately to the hormone insulin.

Hodgkin's Disease
A malignant lymphoma (cancer) characterized by progressive enlargement of the lymph nodes, liver, and spleen, and by progressive anemia.

Hypothyroidism
A condition that causes the thyroid gland not to produce enough of certain essential hormones.

Ischemic Heart Disease
A disease characterized by a reduced supply of blood to the heart that leads to chest pain.

Multiple Myeloma
A cancer of plasma cells, a type of white blood cell in bone marrow.

Non-Hodgkin's Lymphoma
A group of cancers that affect the lymph glands and other lymphatic tissue.

Parkinsonism
Any condition that causes a combination of abnormal movements. These include slow movements, trouble speaking, stiff muscles, or tremors.

Parkinson's Disease
A progressive disorder of the nervous system that affects muscle movement.

Peripheral Neuropathy, Early-Onset
A nervous system condition that causes numbness, tingling, and motor weakness. Under VA's rating regulations, it must be at least 10 percent disabling within one year of herbicide exposure.

Prostate Cancer
Cancer of the prostate; one of the most common cancers among men.

Respiratory Cancers (includes lung cancer)
Cancers of the lung, larynx, trachea, and bronchus.

Soft Tissue Sarcomas (other than osteosarcoma, chondrosarcoma, Kaposi's sarcoma, or mesothelioma)
A group of different types of cancers in body tissues such as muscle, fat, blood and lymph vessels, and connective tissues.

Veterans with Lou Gehrig's Disease

VA presumes Lou Gehrig's Disease (amyotrophic lateral sclerosis or ALS) diagnosed in **all** veterans who had 90 days or more of continuous active military service is related to their service. However, ALS is not related to Agent Orange exposure.

If you have health concerns about Agent Orange, talk to your health care provider or contact your local VA Environmental Health Coordinator (see below) to help you get more information from a health care provider.

Northern Arizona VA Health Care System
500 Hwy 89N
Prescott, AZ 86313
(928) 445-4860 x6436

Southern Arizona VA Health Care System
3601 S 6th Ave
Tucson, AZ 85723
(520) 792-1450 x6173

Phoenix VA Health Care System
650 E. Indian School Rd
Phoenix, AZ 85012
(602) 277-5551 x6749

VIETNAM VETERAN SECRET #1

Surviving Spouses of Vietnam Veterans exposed to Agent Orange

Surviving spouses, dependent children, and dependent parents of veterans exposed to Agent Orange and died as the result of diseases related to Agent Orange exposure may be eligible for a monthly payment called Dependency and Indemnity Compensation.

For instance, if your spouse died from cancers of the lung, larynx, trachea, and bronchus, cancer of the prostate, Non-Hodgkin's Lymphoma, Multiple Myeloma, Ischemic Heart Disease, Hodgkin's Disease, or bladder cancer. It is presumed that they died from Agent Orange Exposure.

VETERAN PENSION SECRET # 16

Home Care Benefits

You do not need to be a wartime veteran to receive these benefits. The program is only for the veteran, not a surviving spouse.

You must be enrolled in the VA Medical System to qualify.

The Home Care Program is a community-based program. For both wartime veterans and non-wartime veterans. It will provide service in the home for activities of daily living. These are:

Bathing, dressing, medication reminders, transportation, meal preparation, transferring, personal care, respite care, light housekeeping, laundry, companionship.

Veterans Directive Care Program

Veteran-Directed Care is for veterans who need assistance with activities of daily living (e.g., bathing and getting dressed) or instrumental activities of daily living (e.g., fixing meals); are isolated, or their caregiver is experiencing burden.

(Source: va.gov/geriatrics/)

This program is based on funding and availability in specific counties. Like the Home Care Benefits, it is managed through the VA Medical Centers.

Ask you VA doctor or social worker about the program and its availability in your area.

How to Apply for VA Health Care

You will need to submit form 10-10EZ, which you can find on our website.

Here's what you'll need to apply:

Social Security numbers for you, your spouse, and your qualified dependents.

Your military discharge information. If you sign in to apply, we may be able to fill in this information for you. If you don't sign in to apply, we'll ask you to upload a copy of your DD214 or other separation documents.

Insurance cards for all health insurance companies that cover you. This includes any coverage that you get through a spouse or significant other. This also includes Medicare, private insurance, or insurance from your employer.

We'll also ask you for this optional information:

Last year's gross household income for you, your spouse, and your dependents. This includes income from a job and any other sources. Gross household income is your income before taxes and any other deductions.
Source: va.gov/healthcare/apply/application/introduction

See References in the back of the book for an approved Veterans Directive Care home care provider.

The Big Mistake!

One of the biggest mistakes that advisors make is not "squaring" their VA benefit planning strategies with ALTCS/Medicaid rules. Someone who might qualify now for Veterans Pension benefits is likely to need additional care at some point in the future. The improper use of financial products that are used to qualify for Veterans Pension could cause a financial disaster if ALTCS/Medicaid is ever needed.

It's essential to work with an expert in comprehensive care planning who understands all the implications of possibly needing Medicaid/ALTCS in the future and who knows how to square the planning with other government benefit programs.

Think of this; if you're having a custom home built and the walls are not square, how stable and sound will that home be? Will it stand up to storms and other natural disasters? Of course not. This same applies to your VA Planning too.

Chapter Sixteen

WHAT IS ALTCS?

Introduction

Arizona's Medicaid Long-Term Care System or ALTCS is a financial safety net for the poor.

Yet, keep in mind that the Medicaid/ALTCS program is also for the SMART!

Steve Dabbs, CMP™

Medicaid is a state and federally-funded program that is administered by the individual states.

Medicaid is the primary payer for long-term care services paying for over 40% of people in America that need long-term care.

ALTCS is Arizona's Medicaid long-term care program. ALTCS is an acronym for Arizona Long Term Care System. It's pronounced ALL-Tex or ALL-Techs.

In Arizona, the state agency that administers the Medicaid program is Arizona Health Care Cost Containment System (AHCCCS).

As a Certified Medicaid Planner™, I'm able to help individuals and families throughout the United States with Medicaid. Here we will focus our attention on Arizona Medicaid and how to maximize the tax dollars you have paid over your lifetime.

In my opinion, Arizona's Medicaid-ALTCS is one of America's best Medicaid Long-Term Care programs compared to other states. It is one of the best long-term care insurance programs there is, an insurance program you have paid for with your tax dollars.

The program is funded by both state and federal tax dollars.

Arizona's Medicaid Long-Term Care System, ALTCS, is a financial safety net for the poor.

Yet, keep in mind that the Medicaid/ALTCS program is also for the SMART!

As is my saying,
"ALTCS isn't just for the POOR it's for the SMART!™"

Those who are wise can preserve assets and still have Medicaid/ ALTCS pay for future care, a spouse, or a loved one.

Even those that need care now, with the help of a Certified Medicaid Planner, can help design a plan that will protect assets and still allow someone to receive benefits under the program.

Chapter Seventeen

IS ALTCS PLANNING BOTH LEGAL AND ETHICAL?

Is Medicaid Planning Legal?

The Courts have answered the question of whether or not ALTCS / Medicaid planning is legal. The answer is yes; it's 100% legal.

In a landmark case, Helvering (Commissioner of the IRS v. Gregory (1934) Judge Learned Hand stated, in the Helvering v. Gregory case, that, "*Anyone may so arrange his affairs that his taxes shall be as low as possible; he is not bound to choose that pattern which will best pay the Treasury, there is not even a patriotic duty to increase one's taxes.*"

The US Supreme Court went on to uphold this decision: see *Gregory v. Helvering*, 293 US at 468-470

In 1996 Congress added a provision under the "Health Insurance Portability and Accountability Act of 1996."

For a very brief moment, Congress attempted to make Medicaid planning illegal.

The law was dubbed the "Granny Goes to Jail Law."

Violators of the law were subject to fines of up to $25,000 or imprisonment for up to 5 years or both. Section 217 of the law made it a crime to: "*knowingly and willfully disposes of assets (including by any transfer in trust) for an individual to become eligible for medical assistance under a State plan under title XIX if disposing of the assets results in the imposition of a period of ineligibility for such assistance under section 1917(c),*"

Then shortly after the law went into effect, in September of 1998, the New York State Bar Association sued the Justice Department and was ruled that the law violated the First Amendment.

Before the Judgement was handed down, then-Attorney General Janet Reno determined that the law was unconstitutional because it violated the First Amendment. She told Congress that the Justice Department would not enforce the law.

Just like state and federal income tax planning is allowed, Medicaid-ALTCS Planning is permitted.

Now, not reporting income is illegal. Just like hiding money and filing a fraudulent Medicaid claim is ILLEGAL, too. On the other hand, converting assets from a countable to a non-countable asset is not.

Is Medicaid-ALTCS Planning Ethical?

How is preserving assets for a spouse or loved one unethical? Is leaving a gift to a church or synagogue somehow wrong?

Remember "My **Why**" at the beginning of this book? I told you the story about the lady who only has $25,000 to live on for the rest of her life.

I dare you to tell her it's unethical to do VA and Medicaid Planning.

Chapter Eighteen

GIFTING IS NOT ILLEGAL

I was conducting an ALTCS financial interview with a client, and the financial caseworker asked a series of questions.

Here is the question I love the most. *"Has the person gifted any money in the last five years?"* I love to say, *"Yes, they did. I told them to do that so I could file the claim."*

On one occasion, the ALTCS worker blurted out, ***"That's Illegal!"***

I responded with this, *"Oh my God. I tell people to do that all the time, I am going to go to jail!"* Then I said, *"You know that it isn't illegal."*

She said, *"Well, no, but it causes a penalty."*

I responded, *"But you just said it was Illegal! Yet you know it isn't. My concern is if you said that to someone that I am helping and now may doubt my ethics or knowledge to help them with their claim. You have no business saying such a thing to anyone."*

I told her that when we were done, I would call their supervisor to let them know what was said. And I called her supervisor directly after the call.

So, what is the penalty? It is a time penalty. One that you can calculate into the application approval

One of the simplest ways to get countable assets below the resource limits is to make a gift to a loved one.

Chapter Nineteen

THE ALTCS ELIGIBILITY AND QUALIFICATION REQUIREMENTS

What are the ALTCS Eligibility and Qualification Requirements?

You can be Eligible and still not be Qualified.

Eligibility Requirements:

- In addition to meeting the financial and medical requirements, the applicant must also meet the following:
- Be a U.S. citizen or qualified immigrant.
- Have a Social Security number or applied for one.
- Be an Arizona resident (See ALTCS Secret #1).
- Age (65 or older or under 18), blind, or disabled.
- Must apply for all other potential benefits, such as long-term care insurance, any pensions, or Veterans Pension benefits.
- Live in an approved living arrangement, such as your own home, or an AHCCCS-certified nursing community or assisted living community or group care home.

ALTCS SECRET #1

You're considered a resident of Arizona the very minute you arrive in the state if you intend to stay in Arizona!

I have helped many people move from other states. They are considered an Arizona resident when they arrive, as they intend to stay here permanently. Many even start the application process before they are physically in Arizona.

This can be confusing because the Arizona Department of Revenue doesn't consider you a resident until you have lived in the state for nine months in a calendar year.

Financial and Medical Requirements

The ALTCS qualification requirements are divided into two parts, these are:

1. Medical and the need for long-term care services
2. Financial requirements

Note that you can be qualified for medical coverage but still not be eligible for long-term care services. Meaning you could be eligible for AHCCCS Medical Benefits and not have a high enough medical need (nursing level) to qualify for long-term care benefits. Or you may be medically qualified but not meet the financial eligibility requirements.

"An applicant needs to be qualified for both medical and financial."

The Medical Qualification Requirements

The ALTCS medical assessment process starts with an ALTCS medical assessor, generally a registered nurse or a social worker, who conducts an interview and reviews current medical records.

They use a 60-point score to determine an applicant's ALTCS medical eligibility. An applicant must be at a nursing community level of care.

The assessment process is called a Pre-Admission Screening or PAS—the PAS takes about an hour to an hour and a half. Because of COVID, the PAS is now being conducted over the phone rather than in person.

The PAS Assessor is required to do the following:

- Interview the applicant.
- Obtain medical information from the applicant's caregivers and personal representative. A family member can be involved with this process.
- Obtain medical records for verification of major medical conditions on all cases and pertinent medical documentation on cases requiring physician review.
- Provide information on the ALTCS program to the applicant and the applicant's representative.
- Provide information about possible alternative services to applicants who may not be ALTCS eligible, like VA Benefits.
- Determine whether a case requires physician review; if so, prepare and send the case for review.

The PAS Scoring process is based on Medical and Functional needs. It is essential to understand that PAS Medical Assessment is a subjective process.

Therein lies the problem with the process. Unlike the Veterans Pension, it is somewhat subjective, where the VA relies solely on what the doctor states in their report. With the VA, if your doctor says you need care, you need care, period.

With ALTCS, it is based primarily on the ALTCS Medical assessor's opinion, who can deny the application. The good news is you can appeal the decision.

Your Certified Medicaid Planner can help by coaching you so you can answer the questions correctly.

ALTCS SECRET #2

Don't lie about your health during the process, but don't brag about your health.

The doctor, hospital, and rehab records also need to support the assessment to be approved.

The Scoring Process

In Exhibit One on the next page, note the three categories on the right. Rating, Weight, and Score.

The Rating is a maximum of three (3) or 20 points, except for Neurocognitive Disorder, where the maximum score is one (1) or 20 points.

Take someone with Dementia; they might be able to take a bath but may need reminders to wash everywhere and use soap. They might only get a weighted score of one out of three or five points.

The same person who is a fall risk and needs stand-by assistance and reminders to bathe but can bathe themselves might have a weighted score of two of the three or ten points total.

At the same time, someone who needs someone to bathe them hands-on would have a weighted score of three or the maximum of fifteen available for bathing.

Sample PAS Assessment

Functional Score	Rating	Weight	Score
Mobility	1	**5**	5
Transferring	0	**5**	0
Bathing	2	**5**	10
Grooming	1	**5**	5
Eating	0	**5**	0
Transferring	1	**5**	5
Toileting	2	**5**	10
Activities of Daily Living (ADL's Subtotal)			35
Bowel Continence	0	**1**	0
Blader Continence	0	**1**	0
Continence Subtotal			**0**
Vision	1	2	2
Commuication/Sensory Subtotal			2
Immediate Environment	0	0.5	0
Place of Residence	0	0.5	0
City	1	0.5	0.5
State	1	0.5	0.5
Orientation - Place Subtotal			1
Day	0	0.5	0
Month	2	0.5	1
Year	3	0.5	1.5
Time of Day	0	0.5	0
Orientation - Place Subtotal			2.5
Wandering - Frequency	0	1.5	0
Wandering - Intervention	0	1.5	0
Self Injurious Behavior - Frequency	0	1.5	0
Self Injurious Behavior - Intervention	0	1.5	0
Aggression - Frequency	0	1.5	0
Aggression - Intervention	0	1.5	0
Resistiveness - Frequency	0	1.5	0
Resistiveness - Intervention	0	1.5	0
Disruptive Behavior - Frequency	0	1.5	0
Disruptive Behavior - Intervention	0	1.5	0
Behaviors Subtotal			**0**
Functional Subtotal			40.5
Medical Score			
Neurocognitive Disorder	1	20	20
Nerological Subtotal			**20**
Summary			
Functional Subtotal			**40.5**
Medical Subtotal			**20**
TOTAL SCORE			**60.5**

Financial Qualification Requirements

Like the Veterans Pension, the financial requirements have both income limits or caps and asset limits.

The Income Cap

Arizona is one of 23 states referred to as an "Income Cap States."

For 2022 the income cap for a single applicant is $2,523 per month of countable income. This changes annually, so be sure to check our website for current income caps.

A handful of income sources are not considered countable, like the Aid and the Attendance portion of the Veterans Pension, which is not countable.

So, if your income is below the cap and you get approved for Veterans Pension with Aid and Attendance, not only does only the A&A portion not count as income, but you are allowed to keep it along with your "Personal Needs Allowance.

This can present a problem because you must spend it each month so that your assets do not exceed the asset cap.

The ALTCS application will be denied even if income is as little as one dollar above the cap. If an applicant's income is above the cap, qualification is still possible with an Income Only Trust -IOT a.k.a. "Miller Trust."

This "Income Only Trust" is flow-through. Income is assigned to the trust, and then income is used to pay the share of the cost of care minus allowable expenses and the Personal Needs Allowance.

The IOT is a carefully prepared document, prepared by either a Certified Legal Document Preparer or an attorney. See Chapter 29; "Do you need an elder law attorney?"

The Income Cap is updated on January 1st of each year, so check our website for the current cap.
See CareFundingSolutions.com/altcs-income-only-trust/

ALTCS SECRET #3

All assets are considered jointly owned by married couples, and all income is separate.

The non-applicant or at-home spouse, technically called the non-institutional spouse, can have unlimited income.

Meaning the non-institutional spouse does not have a cap or maximum, whereas the applicant does. And the non-institutional spouse does not have any financial responsibility to use their income to pay for their spouse's care.

Married Couple Income Calculations

The rule is relatively straightforward with a single applicant. Whereas with a married couple, it can be much more complicated.

The first rule is that there is no need to use an Income Only Trust for a married couple with an income less than double the income cap of $2,523 or $5,046 per month.

Married Income Example #1

Mary and Bob have been married for 42 years, and Bob has a modest pension and Social Security that totals $3,201 per month. Mary only has Social Security of $1,345 per month.

Their combined income is $4,546, less than the $5,046 per month, so there is no need for an "IOT."

Married Income Example #2

Jackie and Bill recently married, and shortly after they were married, Jackie developed Dementia. Bill cared for her for several years until he could no longer provide care.

Looking for funding to pay for needed care, Bill applied for ALTCS. Mary's income is above the income cap, and Bill's income is over $4000 per month. So, the household income total is over the combined total of $5,046.

So, Jackie will need an "Income Only Trust" to qualify.

Here, Jackie's income will be used for care, minus her Personal Needs Allowance and other allowable expenses, and Bill will be able to keep 100% of his income.

ALTCS SECRET #4

SPOUSAL IMPOVERISHMENT

A spouse can get part of the applicant's spouse's income to help with their expenses.

The Medicaid ***spousal impoverishment*** provisions allows for a certain amount of the couple's combined income to be protected for the spouse living in the community.

This the Minimum Monthly Maintenance Needs Allowance, Shelter Standard, and the Standard Utility Allowance.

For example, if the non-applicant spouse's income is low, say $1,300 per month, and the applicant spouse's income is over the limit and an "Income Only Trust" was needed, say $3,200 per month, the non-applicant spouse can get the MMMNA, housing and utility allowance.

The Spouse's Minimum Monthly Maintenance Needs Allowance (MMMNA)

The Minimum Monthly Maintenance Needs Allowance (MMMNA) is the minimum monthly income the non-applicant or at home spouse is allowed to have.

The non-applicant or at home spouse is also given allowances for housing and utilities. These are combined with the Minimum Monthly Maintenance Needs Allowance or (MMMNA), which is $2,177.50 for 2022.

These additional allowances are called the Shelter Standard and the Standard Utility Allowance. Here are **the 2022 amounts**:

Shelter Standard: $653.25

Standard Utility Allowance: $288.00

See website for current figures.

Maximum Monthly Maintenance Needs Allowance

The Shelter Standard and the Standard Utility Allowance are combined with the MMMNA; these three allowances create the Maximum Monthly Maintenance Needs Allowance, which is currently $3,435.

Chapter Twenty

ALTCS HOME AND COMMUNITY-BASED SERVICES

Arizona is an approved Home and Community-Based Services State or HCBS waiver state, and under the HCBS program, benefits extend and include:

- Home daycare,
- Personal and respite care
- Medical transportation
- Mental health services
- Homemaker services
- Attendant care and home health aides.

It's important to understand that the ALTCS qualification requirements are precisely the same whether you stay in your home or a certified ALTCS community or group home. The difference between being in a community or group home is the way care services are provided.

How Much Care is Provided?

How does ALTCS treat the applicant's income?

Let's first review the ALTCS program qualification requirements.

Most know that Medicaid is a federal program; most don't understand that the qualification requirements and benefits vary slightly by state. This is because it is partially funded with state funds and administered by the state.

A state's qualification requirements can be less stringent than the federal rules but not more stringent. Meaning a state's financial caseworker has to follow the federal law along with the state rules too.

Chapter Twenty-One

HIDING ASSETS TO QUALIFY – THIS IS A TERRIBLE IDEA!

Why Hiding Assets to Qualify is a Terrible Idea!

Don't Hide Assets!

Hiding assets to qualify for Medicaid/ALTCS is illegal. This is called Medicaid Fraud. The AHCCCS Inspector General oversees the program to reduce fraud, waste, and abuse of the program.

The Arizona Revised Statute (ARS 36-2918.01) states all contractors, providers, and non-providers shall advise the (AHCCCS) Director or his designee immediately in writing of any cases of suspected fraud or abuse.

Medicaid fraud, if convicted, can result in jail time, probation, community service, fines, and may have to pay back the benefits received.

Medicaid/ALTCS planning is not hiding assets. It is a legal way to reduce countable assets or convert them to non-countable assets in order to qualify for benefits.

Again, hiding assets to qualify is against the law.
Medicaid/ALTCS planning is not!

Chapter Twenty-Two

THE SPEND DOWN MYTH OR THE MYTH OF THE FROG IN THE POT OF WATER

I remember the myth that if you put a frog in a pot of water on a stove and slowly increase the heat, the frog will not jump out of the pot and boil to death.

The truth is that as the water heats up, the frog will jump out, so it is simply not true. It's a myth.

Many also believe that the only way to reduce your assets to qualify for ALTCS is to spend down all your assets on care before being eligible for ALTCS. This, too, is a "MYTH."

See, many will do the same and let the pressure of paying for long-term care heat up before they finally jump and do something!

Every day, I get an individual's call to learn more about ALTCS. The conversation starts like this; *"My father is almost out of money, and he needs to get onto ALTCS. He has been in assisted living for* two *years, and they told me that once he was down to $2000 he could qualify for ALTCS. Now I'm afraid he'll run out of money before he gets approved."*

Like the frog that sits in the pot, they sat and waited until the financial pressure had heated up, and now they are out of money.

Yes, you must have your assets below the asset limits to qualify for ALTCS or Medicaid, that is true.

Spending all your money on care is not the only way to accomplish this.

Seemingly well-informed and well-intended individuals propagate the spend-down myth. This messaging comes from the assisted living community staff, nursing homes, and rehab social workers. It even comes from friends and neighbors, because they are misinformed too.

By looking deeper into the real motivation for so many *spreading* this *misinformation, we might find out that instead of acting in the senior needing care's best interest, which is the standard that I must act under as a fiduciary, they butter their own bread.*

I will let you decide if they are only looking out for themselves, not the person needing care.

ALTCS pays 35% to 50% less than if you pay for the same services. Where the cost of assisted living to you might be $4,500, which I call the retail rate. ALTCS pays a wholesale rate of $2,300 to $3,000.

So, it is simple math. The longer you are on a private pay basis, the more money the community or group home makes.

As I already wrote, *you must have your assets below the asset limits to qualify for ALTCS or Medicaid*; that is true. *But spending all your money on care is not the only way to accomplish this.*

So don't be the frog, don't wait, take action now and jump out of the pot!

ALTCS SECRET # 5

It is not illegal for a family member to pay the difference between what ALTCS pays and the retail rate (what you pay) *with money preserved through ALTCS Planning.*

By utilizing the strategies described in this book, you can preserve assets and then agree with the care home to pay the difference between what ALTCS pays and the normal private pay rate.

Larger corporately owned communities are less likely to agree to this as a strategy, but most group care homes will be happy to have such an arrangement.

ALTCS Planning: Without planning, when you run out of money or just "Spend Down," you do not have any money left to pay for anything.

ALTCS SECRET # 6

"KEEP CALM AND CONVERT"

As I often have said; "Keep Calm and Convert."

Convert Countable assets to non-countable assets and apply for ALTCS.

So here is a short list of conversion options.

___ Pay off your mortgage
___ Buy a vehicle
___ Make home improvements
___ Buy needed personal items
___ Pay off secure debt
___ Set up a formal gifting plan[1]
___ Buy a Medicaid Compliant Annuity[2]
___ Pre-pay final expenses with a Funeral Trust[3]

[1] *See, Gifting is not Illegal.*
[2] See, What is a Medicaid Compliant Annuity
[3] See, Funeral Trust

Again, Do<u>n</u>'t be a Frog: Keep Calm and Convert.

Chapter Twenty-Three

MEDICAID COMPLIANT ANNUITIES –MCA HOW A MCA HELPS YOU TO QUALIFY FOR ALTCS.

A Medicaid Compliant Annuity (MCA) is a Single Premium Immediate Annuity (SPIA, pronounced "speee-ah").

The Medicaid Compliant Annuity, Single Premium Immediate Annuity, has only one real purpose. It is to convert countable assets into non-countable income to qualify for Medicaid long-term care in Arizona called ALTCS.

Once someone takes their savings, IRA, 401K, stocks, and bonds, all countable assets, and uses them to buy a Medicaid Compliant Annuity, the assets are no longer an asset. They become income.

So if someone takes $120,000 and buys an MCA, the asset suddenly vanishes and is now income. The asset is no longer countable. And if married, the income is paid to the at-home spouse and is also non-countable.

Requirements of a Medicaid Compliant Annuity

This amazing financial tool commonly used in Medicaid planning converts your countable assets into a non-countable income stream. **But not all annuities are Medicaid compliant.**

The Deficit Reduction Act of 2005 has set the guidelines for an annuity to become 'Medicaid Compliant.' Medicaid annuities must abide by these guidelines to be considered a non-countable asset.

The annuity must be irrevocable: The parties, terms, and payment amount of the Medicaid Compliant Annuity cannot be altered or revoked. This means once the money is paid, the annuity owner loses control over the countable asset.

The annuity must be non-assignable: The parties to the annuity contract cannot sell it in the secondary market or assign (or transfer) to another person.

We have all seen the commercials. "It is my money, and I want it now!" You cannot sell the contract or income stream.

Fixed annuity term rule: The duration of the annuity and income payout term must be equal to or less than the life expectancy of the owner. The life expectancy should be the same as determined by Medicaid or the Chief Actuary of the Social Security Administration.

No balloon or deferral payments: The annuity payments must be equally distributed to the annuity owner.

Medicaid to be made the beneficiary: The annuity contract must name the state Medicaid agency Arizona Health Care Cost Containment System - AHCCCS as the primary beneficiary, equal to the amount spent as benefits on the Medicaid recipient.

If married, the spouse is the primary beneficiary, and AHCCCS is contingent. Meaning even when exceptions apply, the annuity owner must name the state Medicaid agency as the contingent beneficiary.

AHCCCS is only entitled to payments up to what they actually paid for care. The balance of payments would be paid to the estate of the Arizona Medicaid Applicant.

How is a Medicaid Compliant Annuity used to qualify for Medicaid in Arizona?

Let's explore a few examples of how the Medicaid Compliant Annuity works to help you qualify.

Example One: A Case for a Married Couple to consider a Medicaid Compliant Annuity.

Take Mike and Maureen. They have total countable assets of $274,800.

Mike has advanced Dementia and needs to be in a memory care facility or directive care home for the cognitively impaired.

Mike's income is $1850 per month, and Maureen has a pension and Social Security of $3,400 per month. So, they have a combined income of $5,250 per month.

The average cost for a group home or memory care facility is $6,000 per month.

For Married Couples

Maureen needs about $4,000 a month minimum to live on and realizes they will deplete their retirement savings in less than five years.

$5,200 income
- $4,000 Maureen's living expenses

$1,200 total net income after living expenses
- $6,000 cost of Assisted Living or Memory Care Facility
= $4,800 net negative income

$274,800 Retirement Savings ÷ $4,800 negative income = 57 Mo.

Their retirement savings will be depleted in 57 months!

The Medicaid Complaint Annuity – MCA.

How can it help change this outcome? How can the MCA help by leaving the noninstitutional spouse destitute and paying for her husband's care?

Simple Spend Down Calculation

Medicaid/ALTCS Spend-Down

$ **$274,800**
Total Household Countable Assets**

Community Well Spouse 50% Countable Assets	Spouse Needing Care 50% Countable Assets
$ 137,400	$ 137,400
(Minus) Maximum Community Spouse Resource Allowance*	(Minus) Individual Resource Allowance
-$ 137,400	- $2,000.00
====================	================
$ 0 - ZERO Spend Down	$ 135,400
Spend-Down Amount	Spend-Down Amount

Total Spend-Down is $135,400

As you can see, the noninstitutional spouse or community spouse is allowed to keep $137,400, and the spouse needing care is $2,000, so the spend down required to qualify is $137,400.

Now Maureen and Mike take the $137,400 and purchase a 48-month Medicaid Compliant Annuity.

The Medicaid Compliant Annuity - MCA will produce an exempt income of $2,849, paid to the noninstitutional spouse.

An MCA annuity can also be purchased for a shorter period of time. A 6-month payout would generate a $22,573 monthly income and end in 6 months. This can be advantageous if that asset is not qualified funds. Consult with a Certified Medicaid Planner; remember, Maureen can have unlimited income.

The Six Months Annuity Option

The $135,400 countable asset is used to purchase the MCA and the income is considered non-countable or exempt income.

Now, Mike applies for Arizona Medicaid - ALTCS benefits and is approved for benefits.

Maureen is able to reaccumulate the assets and now has the $137,400 and the payments from the MCA – SPIA total assets preserved:

Community Spouse Resource Allowance =$137,400

Payments from the MCA $22,573 X 6 = $135,483

Personal Needs Allowance (Mike's) = $ 2,000

Total after approval = $ 274,838

Minus planning, income only trust fees, and MCA fees = -$7,000

Total assets preserved = $267,838

Asset shrinkage $274,800 - 267,838 = $6,962!

*(**Disclaimer there are essential steps that must be taken. These steps must be done in the proper order for this strategy to be successful.* ***This is not a Do-it-Yourself project****. Consult a Certified Medicaid Planner who fully understands this strategy and the proper order of the steps in the process.)*

For Single Applicants Needing Extended Care

Qualifying as a single individual is more of a challenge because they cannot shift assets to a noninstitutional spouse. So, they must do what is referred to as (modern) half-loaf planning.

Single Applicant Example: A case for someone single to purchase a Medicaid Compliant Annuity – MCA to qualify for Arizona Medicaid.

Take Bob. He recently lost his wife, Joan, of 50 years, due to complications with Dementia.

Now Bob has about $120,000 left to his name. He needs care but does not want to spend all his assets on long-term care, he would like to leave some money to his niece who both he and his wife love dearly.

Here is what the CMP helps Bob do.

- Bob uses $42,000 to buy a new car so that his niece can use it to pick him up and take him to lunch, the doctor, and family events. He puts his niece on the insurance as a non-owner driver.

The car is an exempt asset, and the State of Arizona AHCCCS does not make any recovery on it when Bob passes (Meaning the state does not make an heir sell the vehicle and reimburse what they paid for Bob's extended care costs).

Now the $42,000 countable asset becomes a non-countable asset - a vehicle. This reduces Bob's countable assets, the $120,000, to $78,000. ($120,000 - $42,000= $78,000)

- Bob buys a Funeral Trust to pre-pay his final burial expenses. He only sets just enough to pay for the final costs, which he and his niece figure would be about $5,500.

This purchase of the Funeral Trust reduced Bob's countable assets from $78,000 to $72,500. ($78,000 - $5,500 = $72,500)

Still, $70,500 is over the current 2022 Arizona Medicaid asset limit.

Step Three: Bob gifts $50,000 to his niece.

Funny thing, when Bob told the executive director that he was going to gift $50,000 to his niece so he could qualify for Medicaid, she told him, "That's Illegal!"

It's not! It only causes a period of ineligibility, that's all.

Arizona Medicaid uses what is called a Divestment Penalty Divisor, which is used to calculate the period of ineligibility that is caused by a gift. The current 2022 Arizona Medicaid Penalty Divisor is $8,029.46. (See the website for the current amount.)

Here, the gift from Bob of $50,000 to his niece will cause a little over a six-month period of time that Bob would be ineligible for Arizona Medicaid benefits.
($50,000 ÷ $8,029.46 = 6.23 mo. or 6 months and 7 days)

Now that leaves only $20,500 left to spend to be qualified for Arizona Medicaid. ($70,500 - $50,000 = $20,500) After the CMP fee for planning and application assistance and the setup fee for the Medicaid Compliant Annuity. (Call for fees and details at 800-543-0530)

This leaves $17,000 to purchase a Medicaid Compliant Annuity for a 6-month period that will generate about $2,840 per month for six months which is just short of what is needed to pay through the ineligibility period because of the $50,000.

Bob now has $2000 in countable assets and can apply and be approved for Arizona Medicaid long-term care.

Summary of the single plan discussed.

Bob and Joan could have started a plan and preserved much of the assets that they had from the sale of their home had they been given the correct information about Arizona Medicaid, as you saw in example one.

Once Joan died, Bob's niece contacted the CMPs at Care Funding Solutions for help.

With the help from the CMPs at Care Funding Solutions, Bob was able to preserve $99,500!

- **Vehicle goes to his niece once he passes** **= $42,000**
  (She uses it now while Bob is still alive, this pleases Bob to be able to help her with a new car.)
- **Funeral Trust** **= $ 5,500**
  (Bob takes the burden of paying for final expenses away from his niece, this too pleases Bob.)

- **$50,000 gift to Bob's niece** **= $50,000**
  (This makes Bob very happy, and he knows Joan would have approved too.)

=========

Total Assets preserved **= $99,500**

*(**Disclaimer, there are essential steps that must be taken. These steps must be done in the proper order for this strategy to be successful. This is not a Do-it-Yourself project. Consult a Certified Medicaid Planner who fully understands this strategy and the steps needed.)*

(See "Gifting is not illegal" video link here)

Something to Think About

Do you not wonder why all the management, past and present, at the assisted living facility are so hell-bent on keeping Bob and Joan from going onto Arizona Medicaid?

Could it be the facility is not approved to accept Arizona Medicaid?

Could it be that the community takes Arizona Medicaid but the State of Arizona pays a lower rate than what the general public does to the assisted living community. Meaning that the community will make less money from Bob and Joan, hurting the corporate bottom line?

Could the community care more about its bottom line than its residents?

All good questions to ponder.

Here is what is sad; many assisted living facilities and group care homeowners will not say one word to their residents and potential residents about Arizona Medicaid as a payor source. I even had one facility in Central Phoenix that is certified to accept Arizona Medicaid, not telling residents that they might be able to get VA benefits or Arizona Medicaid.

I have personally gone by that location several times to get them to let me hold a seminar on VA Pension with Aid and Attendance and

Arizona Medicaid benefits. I was told their residents are cared for and do not need this information.

In 2022, I was called by a granddaughter whose grandmother was a resident at the same facility; she was almost out of her life savings. This was after living there for over ten years and now was going to be evicted!

I helped this resident eventually move to a place where they take Arizona Medicaid, and she is now receiving the care she needs without worrying about money.

Sad, really sad, shame on that facility!

Don't let this be your story. Call us before it is too late and you run out of money. 480-967-8477

How to Set Up a Medicaid Compliant Annuity

Although converting a liquid asset into a regular income stream might sound simple, many complex issues are involved with these types of strategies, such as life expectancy, taxes, beneficiary, and payment rules.

Given the highly technical nature of Arizona Medicaid Planning, anyone interested in pursuing an Arizona Medicaid qualification strategy using a Medicaid Compliant Annuity should seek the guidance of a professional, Certified Medicaid Planner (CMP).

Only an Arizona Medicaid expert can help you correctly understand and guide you in structuring the annuity contract.

Chapter Twenty-Four

THE ROLE OF THE SOCIAL-WORKER

The Social Worker plays a vital role in the well-being of our communities. A social worker with a master's has spent six years in college to obtain their degree.

Here's a typical list of required college courses to receive a "Master's in Social Work."

- History and Philosophy of Social Work
- Social Problems and Social Development
- Social Work Research and Quantitative Analysis
- Human Growth and Development
- Social Work Practicum – I: (Structured Experience Laboratory and Research Methodology Practical)
- Social Work Practicum – II: (Skill Development Assessment)
- Social Exclusion and Inclusive Policy
- Rehabilitation and Resettlement
- Visual Culture
- Social Work Practicum - III: (Concurrent fieldwork - Community Placement)
- Social Work Administration

Interestingly enough, I don't see asset preservation, financial planning, estate planning, Veterans Benefits Planning, or Medicaid/ALTCS Planning as part of their course of study.

Yet they will often advise someone how to qualify financially for ALTCS.

Here, is the advice is just Spend Down your assets, then apply.

Or they start an ALTCS application on their own, sometimes without the person or family even knowing that they did so or any knowledge of their financial situation.

When a social worker does this, it muddies up the claims process and makes it difficult for a CMP™ to help until the claim is denied or withdrawn, causing precious delays in getting the Medicaid/ALTCS application approved.

Valuable time is lost, and the person needing care wastes thousands of dollars in the process.

Remember, over 79% of all ALTCS applications are denied. Is this one of the reasons for the high denial rate? Maybe.

Instead of filling the claim without a complete understanding of the financial situation, the social worker should have the individual or family call a Certified Medicaid Planner™ or attorney to help.

A little heads up—someone in a perceived position of authority or expertise might find themselves with personal financial liability for such action or bad advice. Just a thought.

Chapter Twenty-Five

IMPORTANT LEGAL DOCUMENTS NEEDED FOR LONG-TERM CARE PLANNING

The Estate Plan Documents Checklist

1. Will and Testament

A Will is your declaration of intent on how to distribute your property after your death. The document should specify the person or persons who would inherit your property in the future.

A Will allows the testator to dispose of his/her property in a manner he/she desires. But the right to distribute the property is subject to conditions laid down by state laws. For example, some states provide for spousal rights, which prevent the testator from excluding or disinheriting the spouse.

In the Will, you could include tangible assets (physical possessions like car, furniture, etc. and real estate like a house, farm, etc.) and intangible assets (such as stock market shares, bonds, bank accounts, etc.). The testator can name anyone (family members, friends, or even NGOs) as the beneficiary in the Will.

The problem with only having a will is that it's a guaranteed ticket to probate.

2. Durable Power of Attorney

The Durable Power of Attorney allows you to appoint an Agent or Proxy who would manage your properties, fulfill your financial responsibilities, and make decisions regarding your medical care. The

Agent will act on your behalf and make decisions when you can't do it yourself due to physical or mental incapacitation.

The responsibilities of the Agent could range from paying bills, running the grantor's business, defending in a court of law, deciding whether the grantor should be sent to a medical institution or care home, etc.

It's also within the Proxy's power to use your assets or proceeds from the assets to pay for your medical care. An individual can create a durable power of attorney at any age. Your family members or friends would be forced to approach a court to decide on property management or medical care if you fail to create a durable power of attorney now. The court process might prevent you from receiving immediate care. Plus, the court may appoint an Agent (you would consider unsuitable) or take steps which may be against what you wanted.

The durable power of attorney is valid only if created by a person of sound mind.

The documents can be so worded to give immediate effect of the POA. Alternatively, the Agent gets his/her power to act on the happening of an event mentioned in the document.

The principal can revoke the DPOA at any time unless he/she becomes mentally incapacitated.

Normally, the spouse or children are named as the POV. But the principal can name anyone, for example, a doctor, friend, lawyer, etc. Sometimes, this decision makes sense, because the Agent should have some understanding of mental health, medical care, and financial matters.

You can also appoint backup agents to take up the duties if the main proxy is unable to continue.

3. Trusts

A Trust is an arrangement that offers incredible flexibility for you to manage assets (fully or partially) to achieve certain objectives.

In a Trust, the trustee becomes the owner of the property. The trustee must use the assets or proceeds from the trust assets for the benefit of one or more beneficiaries.

The trustee derives powers from the provisions of the trust document. They must perform functions according to the provisions of the contract.

The grantor can name anyone as the trustee. This includes a bank, lawyer, or corporation, etc. In a trust, the beneficiary and trustee can be the same person.

A Living Trust is created during the grantor's lifetime. The Living Will document must mention how the grantor's properties are to be handled after their death.

The trust can be revocable or irrecoverable. A revocable trust can be changed or revoked at any time by the grantor. That said, the grantor must be of sound mind to create, change, or revoke the trust.

A trust can help an individual realize goals that would be hard to achieve without a special arrangement.

For example, through a trust deed, an individual can make arrangements for property management in the event of physical or mental incapacitation.

You can also create special trusts to transfer certain assets to become eligible for means-tested governmental assistance.

Unlike a Will, the Trust doesn't go to Probate Court to be settled.

4. Beneficiary Designations

You're entitled to receive benefits from retirement accounts (for example, Individual Retirement Account (IRA) or Roth IRA). The retirement scheme allows you to name a beneficiary who would receive the benefits after you. Similarly, some other programs and schemes allow you to name beneficiaries.

You can pass on these benefits to others without expressly adding them to your Will. These assets will skip the probate process, thereby reaching the intended beneficiary directly after your death.

These are collectively called the non-probate assets, and the assets in this category include insurance policies, pension plans, 401(k) accounts, etc.

To keep these assets outside probate, it's essential to name a beneficiary during your lifetime. Wherever you have an asset that you don't want to mention in the Will, and also want to skip probate, make sure you name a beneficiary to that asset.

It's also prudent to name a contingent beneficiary for such assets. Failing to name a beneficiary will result in the court stepping in to manage the asset and deciding on its devolution.

The beneficiaries named in non-probate assets must be mentally sound and over 21. The matter will reach court if the beneficiary fails to meet any one of these two conditions.

It's inadvisable to mention non-probate assets in your Will. Otherwise, the beneficiary designations will get precedence over the person mentioned in the Will. Adding non-probate assets to the Will is bound to result in confusion. The beneficiaries (one mentioned in the non-probate asset and the other included in the Will) may take the matter to the court, which defeats the whole purpose of creating an estate plan.

5. Letter of Intent

A Letter of Intent or Letter of Instruction is an informal document that is not part of a Will. It's a set of instructions from an individual to a beneficiary or executor to be carried out after his/her death.

The letter of instruction may be about anything, including property management, financial information, medical or long-term care arrangements, funeral arrangements, etc.

The document could include anything; behavioral expectations, the individual's life lessons, etc. Bear in mind that a letter of intent isn't a substitute for a Will, and it's not legally enforceable.

As we mentioned, anything can be written down in a letter of intent. Plus, you don't need the assistance of an attorney to create a letter of intent. That said, for the document to help the estate planning process, the following can be included:

- An inventory of assets, both tangible and intangible, is made to help the executor with the distribution of the property.
- Instructions on the location where the individual wants to be buried, the customs to be followed, or whether to donate the body to a medical institute.
- List of personal documents in possession and the location where they are kept. The personal documents could include SSI statements, the marriage certificate, and the birth certificate.
- Address and contact information of beneficiaries, life insurance agent, attorney, etc.
- Location of the other documents included in estate planning.
- Account details and access information of your email, social media accounts, or other digital accounts.
- Information about safety deposit boxes, stock certificates, credit cards, bank accounts, and other financial accounts.

Although strictly not necessary, a letter of intent greatly helps the executor to carry out his/her functions.

It may provide answers to questions the beneficiary, friends, and family members of the deceased may have about the Will and other documents in the estate plan.

If for some reason the Will is contested, the letter of instruction may help the court understand the wishes and intentions of the deceased.

6. Advanced Healthcare Power of Attorney

A lot like the DPOA, a Healthcare Power of Attorney is a document that provides instructions on medical care if in the future you're not in a position to make those decisions yourself. The Healthcare Power of Attorney would normally have two parts:

7. Living Will:

In the event of incapacitation, the Living Will provide answers to questions on treatment options, medications, end-of-life care, etc.

8. Healthcare Power of Attorney:

An agent would be appointed who is responsible for making crucial medical decisions if you're unconscious, in a coma, or become mentally unstable.

You can plan for every eventuality. That said, you're placing your life in the agent's hands. Hence, chose a person who is trustworthy, capable of making the right decisions, knows you well, and shares your views.

The purpose of creating an Advanced Healthcare Power of Attorney would be defeated if the agent is unavailable when the person's service is needed. Hence, name a backup agent who would take the place if the initial pick is unavailable.

9. Guardianship Designation:

The designation of a guardian is as important as a Will or POA in estate planning. You can designate a guardian, which is a legally binding role for two purposes:

- Authorizing someone to take care of your minor grandchildren in the event of your death.
- To choose someone as your guardian if you're unable to take care of yourself due to incapacity or disability.

In some states (for example, Texas), it's possible to assign a guardian for a person or choose a person as guardian for property (estate).

Many people overlook this part of estate planning. They give preference to the durable power of attorney and healthcare power of attorney and forget about guardianship designation. But the designation of guardian overrides the former two documents; hence, it is as important or more important than the two in estate planning.

For example, in the case of unmarried couples, failure to appoint the partner as guardian could lead to complications later. If one person is incapacitated, the other may have to fight a custody battle with a family member (of the partner) in court. A guardianship designation would allow the partner to take care of the incapacitated person and his/her estate without any delay.

The guardian is obligated to act in the best interest of the adult ward. Even so, you need to exercise good judgment while selecting a guardian.

This is not intended to be legal advice.

You could take the assistance of an estate planning expert or attorney, who would advise on the responsibilities of the guardian and factors to consider when screening potential candidates.

Chapter Twenty-Six

DO YOU NEED AN ELDER LAW ATTORNEY IN ARIZONA TO HELP WITH ALTCS PLANNING?

There are situations in which an attorney plays a vital role. These are:

- Complicated Guardianship Cases
- Large Probate Estates and distribution challenges
- Redressal with nursing home issues
- Elder Abuse

This list of legal issues may seem relatively short; the reason Arizona citizens have a viable alternative to hiring a high-cost attorney.

In 2003, the Arizona Supreme Court approved the Certified Legal Document Preparer program or CLDP. This allows someone to prepare legal documents without the supervision of an attorney.

A Certified Legal Document Preparer is prohibited from giving legal advice or recommendations.

Currently, there are a handful of states that have similar legal document preparer programs like Arizona.

ALTCS planning does not require an attorney to help with the process.

There are situations when an attorney may be needed. If you are working with a competent advisor, they will know when to refer you to an attorney for assistance.

Chapter Twenty-Seven

A MESSAGE TO THE ASSISTED LIVING MANAGERS AND GROUP HOME OWNERS

I often make introduction calls to assisted living communities throughout Arizona. I had approached one such ALF community in Mid-Phoenix on several occasions. Each time I dropped by, I heard they didn't need any help. **"All our residents are fine."**

Then one day, I got a call from the granddaughter of one of the residents in that same community. She told me that her grandmother had lived in that community for over ten years and was about to run out of money.

I was shocked to learn that her grandmother was a WWII veteran and that she could qualify for Veterans' Pension Benefits.

So here is a veteran of World War II that could have been getting VA benefits for ten years at the same place that said their residents didn't need any help. The community staff cost their resident well over $200,000 in lost benefits because they did not inform her or her family of their potential VA benefits. **This is a sad story but a true one.**

You play an essential role in helping families manage the cost of long-term care. I believe it's your fiduciary responsibility to inform your residents and prospective residents of the benefits that may be available to them.

I can help by developing legal planning strategies that allow those needing long-term care who might not otherwise qualify for benefits to qualify.

I would be honored to speak at your community, association or club meeting.

Please contact my office for help and ask for Steve Dabbs, CMP™
855-VAPension or 855-827-3674

Chapter Twenty-Eight

MY FINAL WORDS

Helping those with both non-crisis and crisis long-term care planning and assisting veterans with the Veterans Pension and Arizona Medicaid benefits over the past 18-plus years has been the most fulfilling aspect of my career.

As you can now see, finding and paying for the proper long-term care can be a daunting and challenging task. It is essential to seek the help of professionals like a Certified Medicaid Planner™, a Certified Document Preparer, a VA-Accredited Claims Agent, and a Certified Placement and Referral Specialist. Trying to do this on your own can be a costly mistake.

The Elephant in the Room

I charge Arizona Medicaid planning and consultation fees for my service. My fees are one-third to half what a law firm charges for the same service and are allowed and are part of the spend-down or asset conversion process.

Don't Spend Down, Convert.

Think of my fee as converting a countable asset into a non-countable asset or service. My service fee is money you will spend on care anyway, but my service will help preserve assets and save time.

The fee you pay will save you thousands of dollars and untold hours trying to do this on your own. As I like to say, "You're going to spend down assets to qualify anyway, so you might as well use some of it to hire help and save time."

Thank you very much for buying and reading my book!

Please leave a comment on the website:
CareFundingSolutions.com/book

RESOURCE DIRECTORY

Arizona Care Alliance
Local **Care** Resources and Listings
ArizonaCareAlliance.org

All About You Senior Services
Senior Placement Assistance
Phone: 480-498-2277
www.aayss.com
info@aayss.com

Arizona Association for Home Care
www.azhomecare.org
Phone: 480-491-0540

Area Agency on Aging, Region One
1366 E. Thomas Rd, Suite 108
Phoenix Arizona 85014
Phone: 602.264.2255
Toll Free: 888.783.7500
www.aaaphx.org/
Email: info@aaaphx.org

Alzheimer's Disease & Related Dementia Education & Referral Center
Phone: 800-438-4380
www.nia.nih.gov/health/alzheimers

Arizona Assisted Living Homes Association - AALHA
Phone:
https://aalha.org/

Hospice Organizations
nhpco.org/find-a-care-provider/

ALTCS Home Care Provider

Total Care Connections
TotalCareConnections.com
480-387-1927

Long-Term Care Insurance
www.longtermcare.gov
also, see ArizonaCareAlliance.org for local agents licensed to sell long-term care insurance

Medicare Advantage and Supplements

Also, **see ArizonaCareAlliance.org** for local agents licensed to sell Medicare Products

ALTCS.org
Complete ALTCS Provider Guide
Online Only

Listing of ALTCS
Certified Group Homes
and Assisted Living Communities

Arizona Medicaid information

Alzheimer's Association
340 E Palm Ln #230,
Phoenix, AZ 85004
Phone: 800-272-3900
AHCCCS – ALTCS
602-417-6600
Arizona in Home Care Assoc.
AZNHA
Phone: 602-283-3503
aznha.org

Care Funding Solutions
480-967-8477
CareFundingSolutions.com
ALTCS and Veterans Pension benefit information
Caregiver Support Groups

Caregiver Action Network
www.caregiveraction.org/

Legal Document Solutions
602-672-1550
LegalDocumentSolutions.com

Family Caregiver Alliance
www.caregiver.org

National Alliance for Caregiving
www.caregiving.org

VeteransPension.com
Veterans Benefits
855-VAPension

Veterans Directive Care Program
Provider & Veteran Home Care Approved agency.
www.totalcareconnectons.com
480-387-1927

References Material

Certification for Long-Term Care - Reference and training material

https://www.medicaid.gov/

42 U.S Code § 1320 - 1396

https://VA.gov

Title 38 of the U.S. Code

M21-1 Adjudication Procedure Manual Department of Veterans Affairs

This book should not be utilized as a substitute for legal, accounting, or professional advice. If legal advice or other expert assistance is required, the services of a qualified professional must be sought.

Even though Steve Dabbs is a professional and aware of the law, he does not practice law and does not give legal advice.

"We cannot control everything in our lives. Long-term care planning is one thing we can control."

Steve M. Dabbs

Made in the USA
Las Vegas, NV
09 October 2022

56806507R10089